Empowered

2023 Poetry Collection

Empowered represents our student authors as accurately as possible.
Every effort has been made to print each poem
as it was submitted with minimal editing
of spelling, grammar, and punctuation.
All submissions have been formatted to this compilation.

Published by
The America Library of Poetry
P.O. Box 978
Houlton, ME 04730
Website: www.libraryofpoetry.com
Email: generalinquiries@libraryofpoetry.com

Printed in the United States of America.

THE AMERICA
LIBRARY OF POETRY

ISBN: 978-0-9966841-9-4

Contents

Poetry by Division

Empowered

... In memory of RE Carter
(September 26, 2007 to June 5, 2023)
(Student Author)

Pride In This Country
by RE Carter

I am something you see in times of need, the reason many sacrifice
You don't see me much anymore, but I am alive and well amongst many
Lots of people seemed to have lost me, but those who still have me are proud
I was there in 1776, Omaha in 1944 on those beaches
I was there when those towers fell and many came together
I've been alive over 200 years and I will thrive for many years to come
I've been there through the sad times, the hard times and the good times
I'm the reason many have fought for
And even though you don't see lots of me anymore
I am still Alive
I am American Pride

... In memory of Mateja Turner
(December 30, 2003 - February 21, 2023)
(Student Author)

My Trumpet
by Mateja Turner

In the band room lays a trumpet. There are chairs in a neat row.
Stands with sheet music. Lockers with great instruments inside.
The greatest instrument of all is the trumpet. It's a graceful sound when played right.
It's a calming sound. It's a beautiful melody. It's a happy tune.
It is one of the loudest instruments in any band.
It's a shimmering gold that shines in the light.
Some are a wonderful silver. But mine is a shining, sparkling gold.
It kind of tastes like metal.
The bad thing about trumpets is when you can taste the valve oil
as you inhale before playing.
You can taste the spit flying through the mouthpiece.
As you play, you can smell the metal of the trumpet and other instruments.
The smell of sweat is a sign of hard work. It's really not the best smell
This pride at its finest, my mind's voice being brought out in a loud outburst
My heart pouring out a hole, through the air for people to love
The melody of a trumpet

Foreword

There are two kinds of writers in the world.
There are those who write from experience,
and those who write from imagination.
The experienced, offer words that are a reflection of their lives.
The triumphs they have enjoyed, the heartaches they have endured;
all the things that have made them who they are,
they graciously share with us, as a way of sharing themselves,
and in doing so, give us, as readers, someone to whom we may relate,
as well as fresh new perspectives
on what may be our common circumstances in life.
From the imaginative,
come all the wonderful things we have yet to experience;
from sights unseen, to sounds unheard.
They encourage us to explore the limitless possibilities
of our dreams and fantasies,
and aid us in escaping, if only temporarily,
the confines of reality and the rules of society.
To each, we owe a debt of gratitude;
and rightfully so, as each provides a service of equal importance.
Yet, without the other, neither can be truly beneficial.
For instance, one may succeed in accumulating a lifetime of experience,
only to consider it all to have been predictable and unfulfilling,
if denied the chance to chase a dream or two along the way.
Just as those whose imaginations run away with them never to return,
may find that without solid footing in the real world,
life in fantasyland is empty.
As you now embark, dear reader,
upon your journey through these words to remember,
you are about to be treated to both heartfelt tales of experience,
and captivating adventures of imagination.
It is our pleasure to present them for your enjoyment.
To our many authors,
who so proudly represent the two kinds of writers in the world,
we dedicate this book, and offer our sincere thanks;
for now, possibly more than ever,
the world needs you both.

Paul Wilson Charles
Editor

Editor's Choice Award

The Editor's Choice Award is presented
to an author who demonstrates not only
the solid fundamentals of creative writing,
but also the ability to elicit an emotional response
or provide a thought provoking body of work
in a manner which is both clear and concise.

You will find "Mother"
by Carson Kramer on page 217 of Empowered

2023

Spirit of Education

For Outstanding Participation

Peñasco Elementary
School

Hope,
New Mexico

 &

Somerset College
Preparatory
Academy

Port Saint Lucie,
Florida

Presented to participating students and faculty
in recognition of your commitment
to literary excellence.

Division I

Grades
3-5

In Day Or Night
by Abby Crabb

In the day and the night
I'll see you in the light,
even if you're not here,
you are still right here in my heart.

I Love You
by Briley Birkinshaw

I love you so much and I want you to know
that I love you from head to toe.
From your beautiful eyes to your long beautiful hair,
I love you just about everywhere!

The Number One Teacher
by Alexa Hurwit

This poem is about a special person
Who is in my heart no matter what
Over the two years she taught us a lot
Even if some lessons weren't fun
She would always give it a run
She is always very kind
Which is a hard trait to find
She goes above and beyond for all us kids
Mrs. Lleras you are a great big win
- Dedicated to Mrs. Lleras

I Am From
by Ciana Simoniello

I'm from Bounce
From Dodgeball and arcade games
I am from Bounce for my birthday parties
from the corn dogs, pizza and churros
I'm from a China cabinet and pictures of my mom and flower vases.
From Christine and Christy
From "Good morning Sus-Banana"
and "Good morning Sunshine!"
From "Yes, Ciana" and white noise for my baby sister, Aria.
I am from Virginia,
from Adventure land and fun.
I am from going out for my birthday to get food
and Clue with murder mystery.
I am from Grandma's special vase,
from Luciana and Aria.
I am from Disney World with water park rides
from "Mmm ... that's so good!"
I'm from a close and loving family

Life
by Andrew Lareche

Life is fair
Fair for everyone
Life is equal
Equal for all

Snowstorm
by Jackson Smoke

One little snowstorm coming fast
One little snowflake going past
All the people came to see
The little snowstorm over me.

Baby Fox
by Brynn Hartman

To the fox, oh baby fox you are so cute,
the way you crawled up into my lap,
you fell asleep and you had a nose whistle soothed my mind.
You could have bitten me but you did not.
I brushed my fingers through your thick and luscious fur.
You smelt like the wet dirt you find when it stops raining.
You had a puffy tail that would not stop blowing in the breeze.
Farewell fox. It was fun while it lasted,
I will call you Skye, because of your bright ocean blue eyes.
Goodbye Skye.

My Best Friend Maple
by Cayden Monroe

My best friend is not what you think,
She is a sweetheart but boy can she stink.
I was a little nervous when we first met,
But she turned out to be the perfect pet.
Her name is Maple and she makes me happy,
I laugh when she runs and her ears get all flappy.
She broke through the gate,
Which my mom really did hate.
Maple was only trying to find food,
And as she walked past the cows, they moo'd.
I got a bucket of grain
before my mom went insane.
Maple loves scratches on her back
And she does not quack.
She is a rusty red, not blue.
Have you guessed what she is from all of my clues?
Maple isn't a donkey but she is big,
She is my best friend, my 4-H Pig!

Tyler
by Tyler Winike

T is for truthful right from the start
Y is youth, so witty and smart
L is for loving and he's so debonair
E is for energy and plenty to spare
R is for riches precious like gold
Tyler has such enthusiasm and stories to be told

That Feeling of Woe
by Juliana Olonia-Cruz

The cemetery is one we cannot control,
The bodies come and go
The loved ones are gone.
You cannot move on
Because you are filled with woe.
As you wear a black bow to the funeral,
You hear the melodious crows.
You might still feel that woe,
As you grow,
It's natural.

Dream
by Lauryn Mai

What do you want, what do you need?
My animals need some water and feed.
What makes you joyful, what makes you happy?
What makes me happy is my animals to be healthy.
What is your skill, what are you good at?
Not letting my animals get so very, very fat.
What will you look for, or what will you see?
I will see my animals be ever so free.
What is your job, what will you be?
I will be a zookeeper.

What Happens When Your Teeth Aren't Brushed
by Malinda Turman

What happens when your teeth aren't brushed?
Do they sting like a jellyfish sting?
Do they howl in pain like a wolf at the moon?
Do they ooze like a dead body?
Do they weaken like a loose tooth?
Do they get sour like sour candy?
Do they decay like old guts?
Do they wilt like a dying flower?
Do they charge with pain like bulls?
Do they clash into each other like racing cars?

Spring
by Zaida Patterson

Sunny days everywhere
Playing at the park
Raining all day as the sun goes away
Ice cream is amazing
Nice weather, spring flowers
Green grass everywhere

Name Doesn't Matter
by Ariel Doan

If a rose was called trash,
would it smell bad?
If a pillow was called a rock,
would it be hard?
If soap was called dirty,
would it be filthy?
It a shirt was called ugly,
would it look hideous?
It doesn't matter what it's called,
it matters what the qualities are.

Outside My Back Door
by Leona Bryant

Outside my back door I see some
Grass, a tree, 2 bunnies, a snake
Oh, wait, a snake OH NO, OH No
Oh a snake, I can Never catch
A break
Outside my back door I see a swing
Some bling a bench a French oh
Wait some bling it might be ring
Outside my back door
I see ...

A Special Season
by Autumn Davis

Autumn is the season I love the best.
Now some might call me a little bit obsessed,
but I can't help my love for this amazing season.
You would be shocked for this surprising reason.
It's not the leaves that change color each day,
though watching them fall reminds me of the ballet.
I love the cool air that comes from its start,
but that's still not the reason I keep Autumn at heart.
Do you want to know the reason that still remains?
It's because Autumn is also my name!

People's Rights
by Emily Jeanite

Back then people saw signs everywhere
Black couldn't be with whites
and whites couldn't be with blacks
Dr. King had a dream to change that
What he did changed the world for you and me

Summer
by Julia Gear

The sun is shining and I want to play
there is nothing to do today
today is summer and that is true
let's go to the beach! The ocean's blue
It's very hot and I want a fan
So I walked up to the ice cream stand
I told the man "Just vanilla please"
while I was waiting the pollen made me wheeze
I took the cone and then I say
"Thank you for this cone today!"

You Are Different
by Joshua Ng

Do you ever feel different?
Maybe because of your skin color.
Maybe because of which gender you are.
Or maybe because of which race you are.
But no matter how hard you try,
You will always be different.
However, remember that you are you,
You are unique in your own way.
Even though the world can seem big,
No one can replace you.

My Morning Routine
by Trig Eiring

Slam' the alarm off early morning rise
Grab clean clothes, try to open my eyes
Turn on the shower, I am now awake!
The power button on my toothbrush
starting to shake!
Slap on my mousse, style it in
Grab my bag and head out with a grin
Dad yells, "Buckle up, let's go!"
We just go with the flow
Hop out we're at school, don't you know?

A Nurse
by Piera Cassara

So much depends upon
a nurse working with babies
going back and forth
getting measurements right
oh how much depends upon
a nurse working with babies

To the Park
by Brandon Demmons

Mom took me to the park
When I was young
I first went to the playground
I loved the ultra fun slide
It was an amazing trip
Mom took me to the park
When I was young
I went to the swing
I didn't dare touch the deadly seat
It was an awful trip

Who I Really Am
by Emma Marra

I am a gamer
I play all day
Everyone shames
I'm a singer spreading my hope to the world
I am truly a comedian
I go around ascendian
I'm a great dancer, I move my feet to the heat
I'm a makeup artist, I'm adored by everyone
I'm a fighter, I fight for my rights to slay

Sunny Days
by Anya Dash

Sunny days are the best;
Especially when you're in the west.
You can see all the mountains and the trees;
There are also many flowers and bees.
The pine cones, you know there is a ton;
I pick them on the trails and have lots of fun.
The lakes all shimmer from the shining sun;
The boats do come out and so does everyone.
Though the sunny days will come to an end;
But there is still next year to play with our friends.

Our Freedom
by Euree Ann Lee

We don't have freedom, but that's okay,
because we have love without any hate.
We can drive away hate, with our love,
but with punching and fists is all wrong.
We now gather around with our hands together,
we thank our person, savior of freedom,
Martin Luther King Junior,
The person, the one.

Being a Speed Cuber
by Darcy Sullivan

I want to be a speed cuber.
A super, speedy solve.
Click, clang, cleecks.
The cube makes some squeaks.
I want to be a speed cuber.
I want to win with all my might,
But I want people to have no fright.
I want to be a speed cuber.
It has always been my dream.

I Am
by Christopher Bulinskyi

I am a student who is smart
I like to learn things small and large
I'm an artist with an imagination
open wide must to go
They call me funny gamer but I ain't the best of the best
I'm a reader like a leader
I'm a son like number one
My friends call me funny child
I call myself number one

Bindi Irwin
by Poppy Kis

Kind, loving, cool, awesome
Daughter of Terri and Steve Irwin, sister of Robert Irwin
Loves echidnas, family, and animals
Feels happy and excited to see animals
Needs animals, love, care, and wildlife conservation
Gives love, care, and help to animals
Fears bees, wasps, and elevator doors
She would like to see wildlife conservation, safe animals, and no pollution
Resident of Queensland, Australia

How Nice Mrs. Sass Is
by Kaylee Gigstad

Mrs. Sass is very important to me
She does a lot of work you see
She reads to us every day and then we go out to play
Mrs. Sass taught us three times four
And she does so much more
So now you see how Mrs. Sass is so important to me
Now it's time at last to say thanks to Mrs. Sass

Who Is Ryan?
by Ryan Gonzalez

I am a son
My mom's only one
An artist, yes I can draw
I bring characters to life and so much more
A Roblox gamer is what I like to do
come play with me and I will beat you
An orange belt I wear, whew!
I learn to kick and chop
I keep practicing and will never stop

My Personalities
by Gianvittorio Martino

I am fun
I am kind
I can't even rhyme
I am happy
I am reliable
I am a dancer
and I am not that rideable
I hope you like this poem
even if it does not rhyme every time.

Winter Warmness
by Kadence Kern

Winter is cold
The snow is bold
It brings in coats
Some made from goats
It's not the weather for flip-flops
You won't see a bunny dancing to hip-hop
Hot chocolate is the key
To stay warm in delight
But don't spill it on yourself
Or you will have a big fright

A Colorado Winter
by Lilah Barrs

The snow glows as you sip your hot cocoa
watching it fall down to leafless trees
As the snow starts to cover the ground in a big, white blanket,
It makes you all warm inside
and you want to cuddle up and watch a movie
as you see all the little snowflakes fall down
as the big gray clouds surround you.

Things I Am
by Darren Li

I am a student
with lots of good grades
I am a Lego builder
building cool things
I am a kid
just the only one
I am the youngest
and the shortest
of my family

Pets
by Marlow Jairala

Strawberries are red,
Blueberries are blue.
Dogs are sweet,
And cats are too.
Go to the pet store
And buy some pets,
Then go with pets
And fly all the way to
space, on a flying jet.

Awful Pizza
by Talan Russell

When I was going out to eat one day at a pizza place,
the pizza looked weird and it was awful.
When I took a bite of the pizza,
the cheese fell on my face and it was awful.
When I asked what type of pizza it was,
the person who made it said it was New York pizza
even though it was made in Colorado Springs and it was awful.
When I looked around the awful pizza place,
I found an arcade and that was not awful.

Summer Day
by Juan Pablo Hernández

As I walk in my backyard the sun hits my back
I sit on my chair and then I sit back
It is fresh in the morning, warm in the noon
I love the beautiful birds' long strong tune
I look at the trees and feel a weak breeze
The trees' roots are strong as sun shines day long
As I listen to the meadow's song

The Best of Friends
by Alyson Carnathan

My friends are the best
They fill me with glee
Every single day
We will never rest
Till we are done with our spree
They will save me
I will save them
My friends are the best
And I love them so

I Am Me
by Sammy Plevritis

I am short
shorter than you will ever know
I am shorter than Muggsy Bogues
I am a little brother
But I don't have a grandmother
I am a student
and I like to read science fiction
I am a singer
But I love to hit dingers

Alaska
by Jude Conlogue

This story is in Alaska
the snow in Alaska is like the flow of the waves at sea
and the relaxing igloos is so good you feel as home
or like you are floating in the sky
you feel like you're hugging a soft bear.
And you are playing in the snow?
It feels like a soft cloud.
And you can fish up big salmon
it will be the best life for me.

If I Was a Red Bull Skier
by Collin Krummen

If I was a Red Bull skier
I'd zip through the moguls having a blast,
then remembering how much fun I've had in the past
If I was a Red Bull skier
I'd do a few shoots in my ski boots
I know it might seem scary but I'd be fine as a fox
then I'd do a few rocky cliff drops
Then I'd zoom down the mountain with controlled speed
going where the parks are in need
Then I'd hop off some jumps and pumping through the bumps
I'd do an even bigger jump while doing a misty 7
I'd land right over the hump
If I was a Red Bull skier
I'd hop on some rails round and flat
and there's no doubt about that
If I was a Red Bull skier that's just what I'd do
hopefully my dream will come true

Ode to an Amazing Inspirational Women: Michelle Obama
by Grace Durham

Our first image of a gorgeous black Aphrodite
To inhabit the halls of power with charm,
Mrs. Obama moves over the sacred fields deftly
Reclaiming the realm with feminine form.
Sensuously challenging those who dare deny
Her right to bare her bronze sun-kissed skin
As the queen in a staid pallid white world,
She assumes her role with no hint of giving in.
A worthy image of beauty to accompany a giant of a man,
Mrs. Obama came riding eastward with her sword at her side.
She planned for an agenda about change most would scorn,
As a product of northern honing oil and heartland pride.
And she feared not the hard and awful destiny ahead
For a beautiful black woman in a loveless town;
As she brought her fashion for elegance and flair,
Allowing a gawking world to see her face was brown.
As a Capricorn, Mrs. O keeps her keen focus on success,
Never surrendering to impatience, doubt or hesitation.
Her aim is narrow and exact, skillfully chosen
And moored on a carefully thought out foundation.
So doing she has inspired black women to reach higher
And see themselves as lovely creatures of great worth,
Endowed by God to motivate, teach, feed and entertain,
With her nurturing, an emerging color diverse earth.
May you restore the brotherhood of man!
May the whole world become your fan! ! !

What Am I
by Michelle Amstislauskiy

You ask me what I am
I no longer hide behind my mask
While I'm thinking
something strange happens
words start spinning through my head,
faster than I could comprehend,
then it all becomes so clear,
clearer than a mirror
I'm a writer
I see the teacher explain, I stare and I glare, I'm amazed
I get an assignment, I have to explain
I spend hours and hours making sure they understand,
I make sure that once I'm done, every one leaves with a bigger brain
I'm a teacher
While I'm scanning, it catches my eye
I dive deep and I can't pull back
I'm imagining the character dancing
I'm in their world and then I understand
I'm a reader

Am I Good Enough
by Mackenzie Elliott

You are there, you are at that part, you are at the part where
you're stuck, trapped and defenseless.
The only thing you hear is that one person that is telling you.
The vicious words and actions make you feel unworthy. You start to shake.
You ask to go to the bathroom so you can look in the mirror
and ask "am I good enough?" The mirror does not have words though.
It can help you. You look at her, and her perfect hair and perfect face is there.
Her clothes are perfect and she talks perfectly. Even though you know
her life isn't perfect you know, deeply you aren't even to her level.
Your stomach starts to hurt, and you feel dizzy.
A boy is already stuck to her, talking to her all day,
calling and texting while you are left on the side, with no one to talk to.
Her selfishness has been enough and you are sick of it.
The eyes all being on her, and the lies, the secrets, the attention, it's just it.
It is not to be fixed unless she says it is.
Cause you don't have any words. None. You can't say anything.
A little later that ruthless voice is yelling.
But you start to feel some random feeling of power
You start to believe even harder in yourself.
You throw away all of the words she says and the way she looks at you.
You know if you work hard you will be good enough.
And you go back to the bathroom, look into the mirror and you don't need to ask.
You know you are good enough
To all the girls out there, you are good enough.

I Hear My School Screaming
by London Heldsinger

I hear my school screaming
When the doors are slamming
When the teachers are yelling
a lot.
When the whistles are blowing
and the students are running
to line up and get
get back to class.
When the students are crying
for help from the teacher
to stop the bully
from bullying.
When the students aren't
listening
and the teachers
lose their minds.
They will all get angry
and scream all at once,
YOU GUYS ARE
ALL GOING TO
DETENTION!!!!

Doggie Battle
by Leah Beatty

My battle with my dog was kind of crazy,
She convinced me to play, even when I was lazy.
She wagged her tail with cute puppy eyes,
and I was already chasing her to my surprise.
She grabbed her favorite toy to play tug of war,
and wanted to play with me some more.
She pulls really hard, in the game,
and I only try to do the same.
I throw her toy and she chases it with might,
She may look scary, but she doesn't bite!
She has short legs but can run really fast,
and in no time we were having a blast!
The trampoline is her favorite place to bounce,
If I jump in with her, she is ready to pounce!
She jumps with joy and gives me a scratch,
Then runs to the door, and opens the latch!
She runs out the door, wanting a treat,
So I find a yummy one that she can eat.
"Luna, you're a lunatic!" I say,
It's time to rest, but she wants to play!
Snuggled in bed, ready to pray,
and think about our crazy day!

Just a Girl Who Loves Who She Is
by Isabella Giordano

Horse riding is my thing
and after that I like to drink apple cider
With the wind blowing through my hair,
I hope that every horse knows that I care
I am an actress
I love to practice
I know I'm good, that's why I do it
everything we do I know it's worth it
I know I am a BFFLAAF, that loves to laugh
I am a soccer player, that's why I'm the shocker
I know I'm a sister and I like to play Twister
especially with the coolest brother
I am a student that loves to learn
ELA is my thing and that's why I like to write
Lastly, the most important
I am a little girl named Isabella

Rangers
by Adam Bermudez

I am a Ranger
My team is your only danger
You want to be the best
We'll put that dream to rest
You know how to play the game
We'll put your team to shame
You want the Stanley Cup
You're lucky if you're the runner up
Our team will not rest
Until we are the best
You might practice
Yet we still are the fastest
When we score
We make the crowd shout some more
If you get a power play
That isn't the end of the game today
The crowd will always roar
As long as we soar
To all of those Ranger fans
You have the right to clap your hands
We are fast on the ice
But our shots must be precise
Hockey may give us a rough time
But in the end it will all be fine
No matter how many points you got
We will always take that one last shot
I am a Ranger

Can't Cook
by June Cabana

I love to cook and to bake,
but I am a lot rusty indeed.
I want to learn how to make.
I want to learn how to bake a cake, cake, cake.
It's hard still, I'd say.
I do feel afraid I will burn myself.
I can put my pie on the shelf.
My dad can cook without a book.
He's so good you could not believe it!
Could you? Would you?
I make many eggs.
But that is it.
I cooked an egg and it fell on my leg.
It is not so fun to burn yourself.
I overcooked the pie.
I run, run, run and blame it on my sister.
I hurts, hurts, hurts!
I will be the cooking queen!
I will follow the recipe and do it all right.
Well I might ...

Dogs
by Jack Stadel

Dogs can be many things, my poem is to tell you how dogs can be many things
even bad things but we all still love them.
As loyal as a friend
As happy as a dolphin
As cuddly as a blanket
As protective as a mother bear caring for her babies
As cautious as a fox
As cute as a guinea pig
As fierce as a lion
As nice as a capybara
As trustworthy as family
As excited as a squirrel
As detectful as a detective
As fast as a car
As funny as a comedian
As sleepy as a koala
As energetic as a goat
As playful as a dolphin
As calming as a dove
As heartwarming as a baby chick
As talented as a beaver
As hoppy as a kangaroo
But no matter what we all still love them even without their perfections

Where I'm From
by Sophia Yakubov

I am from Whitestone
from soft, green grass and with big parks.
I am from doing Christmas at my grandma's house.
From making homemade sauce in the big bowl.
I'm from the glass ornament from my grandma
and the menorah we light every year and all the stuffies I have.
From Leela and Maria
from "Get up you have school" and "Pass the cheese"
I'm from the scent of perfume and
the sound of the kitchen oven opening.
I am from eating dinner with all of the family.
From Pennsylvania and the farm with all the animals.
From helping my grandma hide eggs for Easter and playing hide and seek
with all my friends hiding behind the couch.
I am from all the projects from school,
from Rosie and Lisa.
I am from ice skating on my birthday where I would stay to the side.
From "How was your day?"
I am from celebrating Christmas with my family.
I am from love.

School and Why I Don't Like It
by Troy Jacobson

The first reason is this is what it stands for
Seven
Cruel
Hours
Of
Our
Life
Plus whenever I add it makes me sad, sometimes even mad
and that's bad, I said to dad.
Whenever I divide I say I tried
he denies, I guess I lied
I tried to hide then got fried
and cried, I cried.
I subtract, that's a fact
I got tracked and attacked so I packed
I said it's cracked when I unpacked
then got smacked, I'm trapped.
Math is a path, take the other path, which is a bath
take the math and feel my wrath
others take math, take the bath, not the math.
Homework is bad
It kills trees
stop the madness.

This Is Me
by Kyleigh Vickers

I am kind and that's hard to find
I shine like a bright star in the sky
I am a swimmer, swimming across the seas
and that makes me very happy
I am bright and smart, I get good grades
and when I go through tests, it's such a blaze
I am a tap dancer and I make music with my feet
and everytime I tap dance I feel a beat
I am an actress and I love to act
and when people say that I know it's a feat
I am a musician and I play the piano
I love to play and sing in soprano
I am an artist and I love to paint
if you see me paint you're gonna faint!

The Seasons and Your Journey With Me
by Corbin Schommer

The four things I think about all the time never really rhyme
I think about summer, fall, winter, spring
as I look under a rock at something interesting
The leaves are falling all around me as I dance to the spring
A thought here and a thought there
all throughout my year, so come along with me
In the summer we like to think a lot about all the things that are sweet
As the birds are hopping on a tree near me
We sit in the sun as we watch a turtle graze and bring ice cream on the way
Soon summer is done and we're just getting started,
soon it will be fall right before you know it.
Once it's fall you will get calls for Christmas present ideas
right before Thanksgiving
Right before that, though, you will see Halloween and all the decorative scenes
After that, you will have a very filling feast as you eat chocolate
and other sweet and salty foods
As we sleep something white falls to the ground and we realize it's almost winter.
We think and think all about the presents we seek and think about everything
We hope we get that one toy we want or that jacket we thought about all year
When the day finally came, we spring from our bed
and look down the stairs to see a living room full of presents
and wake up our parents to go open presents and say bye to winter
We dance with the bees and sing with the flowers
and look at majestic mountains with awe
And glee, we hear the birds singing and see the snow melting
as happy as we can be
Once it gets hot again, we think about the adventures we had and are calm
We sit back and relax as we think about the years to come
and fall asleep while thinking.

Warrior
by Caleb Conley

What do you look for? What do you seek?
A fire bird with a water beak.
What do you long for, what do you crave?
A water gem in a fire cave.
What do you lack? What do you need?
A fire sword on a water steed.
What do you want? Of what do you dream?
A fire ship on a lightning stream.
What do you have? What do you own?
What would you be? Oh what would you be?
Only the best warrior of both land and sea

Why Is the Night Dark?
by Ella Crowe

Once there stood a flower that was dead
Petals were falling from the head
The stem was all bent in half
But it used to stand tall as a giraffe.
A boy who is very sour
Removed the soil and picked the dead flower
He carried it into lots of sunlight
Because it was dead he thought it would crumble overnight
But that was the only thing he was dedicated to
He did his best to make it brand new
He put his heart into this flower
And before he knew it, it was as tall as a tower
He finally felt joy, he was nicer to kids
He acted like a whole new boy
His friends didn't like it and that made him mad
So he focused on his flower so he didn't feel so bad
He watered it so much that it stretched in the air
At night it went to the sun when he wasn't there
Bugs crawled up it and covered the sun at night
The bug made it up despite the height
But when they got up they burnt on the heat
Man! I feel so bad for their little feet!
The sky was dark so the boy asked his spiritual aunt
He asked her if she could fix it but she said she can't
She tried anyway with all her strength
Her potion reached the sun despite the length
But the flower's pollen got into the sky
So it only made the day light
There wasn't anything else to do
I guess the flower was even better than new!
So after that day, it has always been dark when you go to sleep
So don't love a flower too deep!

Freedom Is Great
by Emily Baranov

Love is great, hate is bad
You should treat other people
the good way they treat you!
People should treat others equal

I Know a Goat
by Lily Roberts

I know a goat who ate a want and a cloak.
He ate a potion that made smoke.
and Hermione, Harry, and Ron, and don't forget Professor McGon.
He spat it all up and what did he get?
7 books and a movie set.

Abraham Lincoln
by Ashlyee Johnson

Mr. Lincoln was a wise working guy
He learned to read and write very well
Lincoln was an Honest Abe
He freed the slaves
Saved the day
Oh yes,
Honest Abe did it all
Mr. Lincoln, Honest Abe, oh young Lincoln
The one who did it all

I Am Strong and Brave
by Aarya Chattoo

I am strong and brave
I wonder if I will do good at the spring concert
I hear the orchestra playing music
I see the crowd cheering
I want to do good at the spring concert
I am strong and brave
I pretend to be a professional violinist
I feel the excitement
I touch the stage
I worry if I mess up
I cry when I miss up
I am strong and brave
I understand that I am not perfect
I say, "You got this!" in my head
I dream that I will become a professional violinist
I try with all of my effort
I hope that I will do good at the spring concert
I am strong and brave

A Rose That's One In a Million
by Alexis Charles

A rose without thorns is like
life without measure,
May all the rest of your days
be filled with love and pleasure.

Halo
by Jameson Kee

He feels fluffy, he feels soft, he feels wet because it rained
He smells like dirt, eggs and dog
He sounds like squeals, barks and whines
He looks like a beagle, doxie, husky and boxer, he is 8 different breeds
He tastes like a dog and fur.

A Starry Night
by Audrey Bobo

As I sit here by the creek
Right under an aspen tree
Looking at the beautiful peak,
Behind me, the forest
Where all the deer flee.
While the wind blows through my hair,
And the stars shine so bright in the night,
All the worries in my mind aren't there,
Try as they might.

Snowy Day
by Abigail Brooks

In the glinting sun
The kids play in the powder
The snow has fallen.
Here comes the blizzard
Of only white and ice shards
Winter has fallen.
Thick layers of snow
Frost has coated all the trees
The leaves have frozen.
Inside all the homes
Families surround the hearth
Cozy by the warmth.
Birds are going south
The bears are hibernating
Squirrels safe in their holes.
As the cold breeze blows
Everyone knows, bear or bird
It's true - Winter's here.

My Balloon
by Alissa Montana

Life's like a balloon
Rises up when I'm happy
Goes down when I'm sad

The Fat Cat
by Cailey Stout

A fat cat likes to sing.
The cat's brain went ding!
The cat ate a lot of food.
The fat cat is rude.
The fat cat loves that thing.

My Buddy Oreo!
by Miles Ancevic

My dog Oreo is black and white
Compared to my other dogs,
he is very light
He is so small
I could carry him around in a teacup
He is the family favorite pup
He snorts and sniffles
And it's just as cute
As when his hair frizzles

Distractions
by Gwen Hindman

Have you ever speculated about the media?
Wondered "How long until something new happens?"
You constantly check
Facebook,
Tik Tok
Instagram,
On Monday, you see that Jessica got a new cat
It's Tuesday, anything you saw the day before is replaced with new information
Wednesday now, something big happens and you can't stop thinking about it
When will there be more news about that?
It distracts you,
The small news isn't interesting,
nobody is talking about Jessica's new cat anymore
Everybody is talking about this big news,
and everywhere the concentration is poor.
Over and over again this happens
Over and over in a loop
Over and over,
This life is full of distractions

Land
by Mason Tsering

Grass all over the world
Water is all over the place now
Trees growing big and small

The Rose
by Madilyn Johnson

Once there was a rose.
All she did though was pose.
She went to the store.
She said what a galore.
And then she tickled her nose.

A Night In the Country
by Cora Kampfer

The crickets are chirpin'
The frogs are croakin'
Staring at the stars tonight.
The stars are shinin'
The fire is crackin'
Night's going fast tonight.
The kids are playin'
The dog is yippin'
We're having fun tonight.

The Journey Is Turbulent Without the Lord
by Evelynn Dugan

The Lord is always with us
Through tough and rough,
Through illness, through bad-subconscious
Through so much of our troubles.
He has created a wonderful world,
Where we earn happiness when we strive.
Those with illness always thrive
In their great lives.
Oh, what a wonderful world it is!
One troublesome day,
The Lord sent his son to pay
For the mistake I have made,
But the Lord still comes to aid.
The Mighty One shows forgiveness!
This is where I want to be
Under the protection of my Savior
Who loves me
Oh won't he help guide the way for all who believe?
Oh yes, the Mighty One will!

Snowman
by Kacey Coleman

Always icy cold
near hot stuff they're never bold,
their arms are straight like sticks
they're kind of hard to fix
especially if your sister gives it a very big lick!
They have a carrot nose,
they always have no toes
their buttons are rock hard
and they're almost always bald!

I Am Me
by Olivia Jeanite

I am a reader, a child of books
If you leave, I will not take a look
I will read, and read, and read
but never look up at my mom leaving the house without her key
I am a black child from ancient history
I am from a very long ancestry
I love the way my black skin looks on me
I am a sister, a daughter of two
I am a niece, a cousin, family through and through
I am an artist, a student, a librarian, a friend
But most of all (you can see), most of all, I am me

My Best Friend
by Lila Treworgy

My best friend is moving away, I won't get to see her for anymore days.
I dread the thought of not seeing her again,
when I am with her it feels like it will never end,
the thought of never seeing my best friend again.
On the last day she's here, I want to tell her something,
A few words she'll never forget
I know it will be hard but we'll get through it together,
though I will never see you again, remember we'll be friends forever.
I have an amazing idea that will bring us together
We can be pen pals, I'll give you my address, you give me yours
We'll write long stories and make each other laugh,
until our bellies hurt and we can't find breath
And as time passes, you might not write back and that is ok,
just remember what I am about to say
On the nights when it's tough and you feel like you can't go on,
Read this poem, it will make you feel better
Read it out loud, or in a small silent voice,
Just read it to anyone, it can be your choice
So now that this poem is coming to an end,
I just want you to know you are my best friend.

Axolotl's
by Meara Kautzmann

There's a mysterious creature down in the lake
it's an axolotl don't make a mistake
they are yellow and white even pink
they are not like the missing link
they are rare so they will stare
they regrow legs so they won't lose a hair
I met an axolotl her name was Ranae and she had to say
I love my frills please can I stay
I said ok we went on our way

Look Both Ways
by Samuel Eli Torres Ortega

I come to school, disappointed in myself
Because I "forgot" to do my homework
I turn in my homework frustrated in myself
And I think "Why did I play games?"
The next day I got my grade, "An F!"
I come to school, proud of myself
Because I did my homework and had freetime
I turn in my homework, sure I would get
An A, and think "let's go, keep going"
I chuckle, excited to go to go to school tomorrow
The next day I got my grade, "An A, expected."

Seasons
by Emma Haskell

Autumn leaves falling to the ground,
red, gold and brown.
Drifting through the trees following me, don't you see them following me?
From tree to tree they drift down low, don't you see the red, gold and glow?
These are the autumn leaves.
Autumn gives way to winter, snow and all,
it blows through the trees cold and low,
Sending chills as they flow,
it will blow and blow and blow.
This is winter snow.
After comes spring, when the birds will sing,
when sunshine shines through the day.
Spring will come in the month of May,
and the warmth will make its way.
This is a warm spring day.
Soon comes summer and out comes the hummer.
On this day the sun shines bright.
This season brings light, even at night.
The sun is in sight,
this is a bright summer night.

My Friend and I
by Morgan Reed

I felt the cold, brisk winter air
As your mane moved with my hair,
Jenna led you through the grass.
I miss the days I got to see you,
Now you are no more,
As you leave I stay,
Every time I think about you
I miss you,
All I can say is thank you for being my friend.

A Delay In the Day
by Mavin Goldsmith

I wake up in my room as it snows and snows.
I soon find out school is delayed.
I can finally close my eyes again.
Snow glistening in the air so beautifully, almost like it is dancing through the air.
It's so peaceful throughout the house no one even is awake but me.
I can finally relax and read by myself on the prettiest day of the month.
It's gloomy and yet it is sunny and bright.
I am not yet sure which one it is.
As I stare out my window, snowflakes fall down so gracefully and slowly.
As I sip my water and eat my breakfast, I feel calm and relaxed.
This is such a peaceful morning and I love it.

Bikes
by Owen Wolbert

I have some bikes that are fast
I have some bikes that are colorful
I have some bikes that look cool
I have some bikes that are metal
I have some bikes that are cold
I have some bikes that are hot
I have some bikes that do tricks
I have some bikes that hurt
I have some bikes that are plastic
I have some bikes that are for dogs
I have some bikes that are
I have some bikes that have a car steering wheel
I have some bikes that are tall
I have some bikes that can crash
I have some bikes that are hard to balance
I have some bikes that are heavy
I have some bikes that have big wheels
I have some bikes that can jump
I have some bikes that have shiny petals
I have some bikes that have shiny sterling wheels

I Am From
by Payson Morford

I am from a loud house
I am from late night rodeos
I am from working on trucks with dad
I am from road trips to my uncles
Riding horses until dark
Watching sunsets with siblings
Fixing fences with my sisters
Wrestling with my brother
And that is the place I grew up in ...

Me, Myself and I
by Crystal Aaron

Me, myself and I, soaring through the sky
walking down the street
I scream out "I am beautifully unique!"
I am a poet, letting my words flow
I am perfect, and I top that with a bow
I am a singer, singing my heart out up into the air
I am a dancer, letting my body float up into the air
I am also a gymnast, flipping and soaring through the atmosphere
Finally I am an artist, brushing paint, layer by layer
So me, myself and I, were soaring through the sky
It's time to rest, but all day I tried my best

Talking
by Jazzlynn Quintana

Phone's talk. Videos talk.
People talk in tones.
Animals talk in ways we don't understand.
There are words that are not even there.
It's a muffled sound.
"Hello?" "Can anyone hear me?!"
Noise is all it is now.
Talking is a muffled noise that is there.
A swarming noise that sounds like a tornado.
It roars around you day in and day out.
"Is anyone there?"
Nobody is to be found. It's all gone.
It's just words soaring around you. All kinds of kind or hurtful.
Can you escape all the hatred and rudeness?
You're in a dark place in your life and there's no help.
What hope? What is the cure?
Calmness is completely gone.
What is the point in all of this help I give?
While nothing is returned.
All of the anger in me is bad but I must continue to use kindness.

Waterfalls
by Ivo Patxi Marcuerquiaga-Hughes

Waterfalls shimmer
In the mist of breaking dawn
With a golden sun

US Flag
by Sarah Wang

Stars and stripes,
Mark the land of our forefathers.
Fifty states of freedom and equality,
A beautiful country unlike any others.

My Favorite Things To Do
by Gavin Wagenblast

I like to run, I feel the wind blowing through my body,
when pacing through the sky, while running with my shoelace to the end.
I like being an athlete, I play kickball on the field
I race through the base while keeping my pace with my shoelace
tangling through the wind, when the birds chirp
and the flowers dancing through the wind
as the birds also chant.

The Violin
by Auren Pelkey

A man is playing the Violin in a room all alone.
As the man plays the Violin, he gets lost in his music, very prone.
The Violin seems like a living being.
Yet sitting as still as a spiderling.
As the man plays more, the Violin seems to be moving more than before.
The Violin is now seeming to shake,
but as the man looks at it, he sees nothing but its core.
By the time the man is done playing, the Violin has stopped moving entirely.
It's almost as if the Violin is calling the man, loudly and clearly.
The man sighed, and followed the call, continuing to play.
After hours and hours, almost a day, he still has absolutely nothing to say.
When he finally stops, the Violin still pleads and begs him to stay.
And, yet again he sighs heavily and decides to stay playing.
Eventually, he gets lost in his music, and ends up playing all day and all night.
Yet the man feels absolutely nothing, not even fright.
No hunger, no thirst, no pain, no depression.
As the man plays more and more, it just makes a longer session.
The man ends up playing forever, no start, no end.
Still obsessed, the man fully sends.
The Violin, with no end.
Is still, and always will be, a never-ending friend.

Spring
by Malachi Williams

Spring is so fun
In the sky, shines like the sun
The birds really chirp a ton

Freedom
by Kaylee Flores

Freedom, Freedom, Freedom
We need Freedom
Freedom is great
Freedom can't wait

My Name Is Lydia
by Lydia Valenti

My name is Lydia
My name rhymes with nothing
I am cutting my name and I am naming myself Bluffing
Lydia's not cool, while Bluffing's in a bright blue pool
Lydia's like poop, but Bluffing's like snoop
Lydia's name is nice, but Bluffing's name is like mice
So I'm going back to Lydia, but Lydia rhymes with nothing.

Dogs
by Baylee Davis

Dogs are meaningful to me because when I don't feel good
they always make me feel better by cuddling with me.
I see dogs with accessories all over the world,
I see some with leashes, I see some with collars,
Some with no collar and no leashes,
Some with long tails, some with short, and some with nubs.
I smell dogs all around,
Some smell good, some smell bad, some smell like dog wash.
Some smell like people's houses, some smell like the inside of cars.
I hear dogs all around,
Some bark, some howl, and even some snore
Some scream, some scream and bark
Some even sound like a human
I see dogs all around,
Some are fluffy, some have rough fur, some have none
Some have blue eyes, some have brown eyes, some even have green
Dogs have taste all around,
Some taste like shampoo, some taste like fur,
and some even taste like dirt,
Some taste like the lake, some taste like grass
And even some taste like mud.

Valentine's Day Love
by Gianna Molinaro

Love is the sky, it's everywhere.
Love is the ocean, it has its ups and downs.
Love is the mountains, it can go high.
Love is a box of chocolates, it's filled with good things.
Love is a rose, the petals might fall off, but the scent is always there.
Love is an airplane, it soars the sky.
And that's why, Valentine's Day
LOVE IS EVERYWHERE!

Stars
by Lydia Geist

When I look up into the sky,
what I see is big, bright eyes.
Staring down as I look up,
I need nothing more to fill my cup
Stars, stars, beautiful stars gazing down at me
Stars, stars, beautiful stars, they glisten and they gleam
A look of wonder in my eyes
I gaze up into the night sky
And suddenly I understand
these stars are just like grains of sand
Million and billions though none quite the same
They are so very different, but all shout out their name

Summer Is a Time To Play
by Brody Holtz

Isn't summer so amazing?
I always find myself gazing.
Summer is a time to play,
And I would like to stay.
I want to shout!
No need to pout.
While the sun beats down;
There will not be a frown.
Summer is a time to play;
While the horses all neigh.
The days are so fine;
All of them mine.
Please come down by the shore,
And hear what this is for.
Summer is a time to play,
So close your eyes and let's lay.
Come around the campfire,
So that we can admire.
Summer is a time to play;
To keep invaders at bay.

Fortitude
by Ronan Miller

Sometimes I feel like I can't do anything
But with friends,
Trust,
And last, but not least
Fortitude
You
Can
Do
Anything

Colorado
by Samuel Bohmann

Colorado has millions of trees.
If you are lucky there will be honey bees.
Trees are big and beautiful with leaves.
Bear like honey they steal from the bees, they are thieves.
The Av's have a game full good theme.
The Colorado Avalanche is a team.
The players skate fast, they blow off steam.
The Colorado Avalanche is a dream.
Colorado has many places.
Colorado has many different faces.
They have many flowers for vases.
They have many places for my fun laces.

Why Am I?
by Theadore Russell

Why am I?
I often ponder
perhaps life is more simple than pi?
We aren't shy
to wonder
why am I?
We don't cry
nor somber
perhaps life is more simple than pi.
We aren't shy
to wonder
why am I?
We don't cry
with a wonder
perhaps life is more simple than pi.
Maybe think, try
"Is life to live?" Now don't ponder
why am I?
Perhaps life is more simple than pi.

Hmmm ... What's That Smell?
by Oscar Aldana

Sniff! Sniff! Sniff!
My goodness! Why does that smell so good?
Creeeeeeek ... goes the door.
There's the smell.
I sit at the table.
I can't wait.
Here comes the food.
Yum! So good.

Forever Me
by Pierce Morris

I am a sister
a younger one at that
sometimes I am annoying
they call me a rat!
I am a singer
with a great voice
sings in the shower
I'm a blooming flower.
I am an artist
I try my hardest
get no rest
I do my best!
I am an actor
I want to be on tv
loves Peyton List
Love myself and who I be!

My Amazing Life
by Alaina Haughton

I'm a girl
I rock the world
I'm an artist
I work the hardest but I'm not the smartest
I can dance and do gymnastics
And I can be fantastic
My mama says I've got style
and she really makes me smile
I have a sister
I have a brother
They make me feel like no other
I am strong but sometimes I'm wrong
I flow like the wind
And I play games that I can win
But to tell the truth
Life is the best when there's no stress

Turtles
by Juliana Baca

Tortoise
Land, feet
Lettuce, cute, watermelon
Shell, bumpy, green, eggs
Fish, seaweed, cute
Water, fins
Turtles

I Am
by Norah Paulemont

I am a runner
as well protector
and I'm a need my bling
cause I slay all day
I am a dancer
that reaches for the stars
the sky is my limit
so that where I'm going
I am a mini cook
who takes her time
bar a little too much time
and the food is burned
I am a friend
that likes to sing
calming songs
like a river flows

Beans Travel
by Lisetthe Alfaro

There once were four beans that went on a trip.
They sailed with a ship.
The first bean was on an island where
Everything was made out of hair.
The second bean went out so far
Where there were many guitars.
The third bean went to an island
Where it was mostly dry land.
The fourth bean marched up a hill
Where there was a pile of gills.
They all saw clouds
They were very proud
They looked at the sea
It looked like tea.
They then looked at the ground
It made a funny sound.
Suddenly they fell through the ground.

Purple
by Hunter Uhuad

Purple is a bunch of fresh grapes
Purple is a school of little fish
It is lily pads and gemstones
It is ribbon, string, and paint
Purple is a lavender plant blowing in the breeze
Purple is the joy of life

The Fall of 1775
by Lauren Wong

You may think you have it all
This is what happens before your fall
Happy and cheery, but then become weary
Do you really think that's all?
The American Revolution, for example
Is an exemplary sample
Of how you will fall
If you think you have it all
The British king
Had the troops, the supplies
But the Americans multiplied
From France to Spain
America brought Britain pain
Now, always do your best
To never get stressed
But never let your pride
Mask everything inside

Screens
by Sophia Grace Guzman-Pacheco

I use screens from morning to night,
they give me so much delight
My parents use screens to watch the news,
the weather, the traffic too
They also use G.P.S. to go from place to place
without it, places would be a big maze
My siblings and I use screens at school too
they are one of our learning tools
Their entertainment gives us fun in our spare time
But sometimes screens aren't so kind
they leave all the outdoor adventures behind
There is also less face to face friendships and other physical interactions.
Most of the time we use screens only as a distraction
There must be a way to harness the issue and control
And instead go outside for a stroll
With a balance of connections with our families and friends nothing can go wrong
So may the use of screens stay for long!

Rocks
by Gavin Richter

Rocks are bumpy like bobbing bears
Dusty like digging dogs
Cold like chilling chimps
Crunchy like crumbly crackers
And they look like snails

Sunrise
by Audrey Jacoby

Sunrise in the morning
The earth will continue warming
Beautiful flowers won't decay
When the sun gets in the way
A shining star, up above
Forever, we shall always love
Please, do me a favor tonight
Close your eyes and give a thank, alright?
Sunset in the afternoon
Telling us, "get to sleep"
Pink and orange sky's bloom
Fall asleep, don't make a peep
Space, the place that the sun rests
Don't worry! The sun will come back soon, I guess
Goodnight sun, you too moon
Eyes shut, nice and warm
Listening to my favorite tune

I Live For TKD
by Hunter Kaplan

I am strong and athletic
I wonder if I will ever get on a travel TKD Team
I hear boards breaking and people yelling
I see boards flying
I want to always get 1st place
I am strong and athletic
I pretend to be at a tournament when I am home
I feel I can always do a little better
I touch the boards, medals and trophies
I worry that I won't break the board
I cry when I get 3rd or do not place at all
I am strong and athletic
I understand I cannot always get 1st place
I say "Yay" when I come in 1st place
I dream of becoming a Master
I try to win 1st place in tournament
I hope I will continue to improve at TKD
I am strong and athletic

Rhythm
by Addison Joseph

I love to sing when I'm wearing bling
It makes me feel the best when I put myself to the test
I also love hip hop, people say my steps drop
When the world gives me words in my head
I feel like it's something I've already read
When I walk by a tree, I let out my glee
Rhythm, Rhythm, Rhythm is my favorite thing to sing
Rhythm, Rhythm, Rhythm watch I have sharp bling

The Rabbits and the Pup
by Rhea Garner

Binzy, Binky, Buttercup
Were on a flying carpet
Then they found a little pup
They bought her at the market
Binzy, Binky, Buttercup
Are searching for a carrot
They rolled a ball to their pup
Thin stopped and asked a parrot
Binzy, Binky, Buttercup
Then followed his pointing beak
Sniff sniff went the happy pup
They found the carrot they seeked
Binzy, Binky, Buttercup
Shard carrot 'till it was noon
They petted the lil pup
And then they flew to the moon.

Smile
by Jade Santana

Smile
Put on a mask, put on a smile
No one is going to notice
Don't let them see through the curtains
Don't show them the girl who hides inside
Don't show them the little girl that cries.
Don't show the little girl who cries herself to sleep,
Don't show the little girl who screams inside her head,
Don't show the little girl that hurts herself,
Just put on a smile and fake it all, It's all an illusion.
Just make it seem you're happy, Just ... Smile,
But who is going to help her, who is going to be there for her,
No one. So lonely, no one who understands her, no one to hold her,
no one to tell her she'll be ok, no one to say
"everything will be fine", she's all on her own
Just smile ...

Air Force Academy
by Bode Diskin

I love to study the Air Force.
It will take, it will take.
About ten years before I can, before I can.
I need to study before I get to see my buddy.
We will fly through the Air course.
We fly in the Air to stare at the bear, at the bear.
Welcome to a landing so we can start the fueling.
Then we go back in the Air so we can stare everywhere.

Friends
by Claire Pomeroy

Keep you warm
and cozy so tight
during the darkest storm
and in the darkest night.
Always there
like family
fill you up
with joy and glee.
Live love
and like a pillow,
fragile dove
will sway like a willow.
For we need people to see
people like you and people like me
that places with friends
are the places to be.

Castle of Auld Lang Syne
by Anileh Chen

Moon over ancient castle, quiet is the sight
Beauty now surrenders to the weary night
Sister, look there, at the moon, dancing to no tune
Waiting for a joyous song- or are they all gone?
Silent and forlorn, lies the ruined castle
Resting on a lonely hill, even joy stands still
The moon the only candle on this whole vast plain,
Ringing through the wailing wind: What will end Night's reign?
Yet there is not long to wait, to the moon's dismay
For, behold the first rays, blooming a new day
As on dark the light pours forth, bringing hope to earth
What once gave way to the night, now gives rise to mirth.
Dark and dreary shadows, bid a soft farewell
Light cast on the broken ruins, an auld lang syne tale
'Neath the sunlight glistening on the moat rippling
Now darkness has fled and gone, thus begins the dawn.

One Snowy Winter
by Aspen Campbell

It's winter!
The snow is falling down
I can see it on the ground
It sprinkles and it blizzards, it gives me the shivers.
The windows are frosted
and I get exhausted
The roads are slippery
and I see the burnt hickory.

Brooklyn
by Ava Shahin

Brooklyn
It's home to me
And you will see,
Why it is so special to me
Trees
Buildings
Parks and more
I hear the children playing from door to door
There are so many
Sights to see
And great food to eat
As you're walking from street to street
Brooklyn
Now I hope it is easy to see
Why this amazing place
Was made for me!

I Am From
by Laikyn Brown

I am from the countryside
I am from cows mooing all night
I am from Christmas dinner
Feeling the moist cake as I feast
I am from ranching and
Playing in the mud
I am from dogs
And cats and fish
I am from talking at the dinner table
I am from bad dad jokes
And small giggles
I am from County Fairs
And homemade ice cream
I am from a place with many memories
That will never go away
And that is where I am from

Spring
by Isabelle Luellen

Spring is a fling
I see butterflies open their wings
The bees come out to sting
I come out to play on the swings
I see the sun bling in the spring
I love to hear the birds sing
I hear the bell in the town square ring
Oh why I love spring

Why
by Lariel Stallworth

Why are we people
Why are we here
Why do we breathe
The atmosphere
Why do we laugh
Why do we cry
Why do we get
Sand in our eye
Why can't we
Live underwater
Why can't we
Stay a little longer
Why can't everything
Go our way
Why don't we
Just rest for the day

Storm
by Evangeline Allen

I can hear the split, splat, splash
of rain hitting gravel roads.
And the rumbling of the thunder above
the gray, gloomy storm clouds.
I can feel the breeze of the harsh
storm blowing against my rosy cheeks.
And the gentle tapping
of rain on my shoulders.
I can see the sudden flash of lightning,
striking out of the unclear sky.
And the little droplets of rain slowly
filling cracks in my driveway.
The storm rolls over as the sun
peeked through the black, heavy clouds.
To shine bright on all that is below,
To give us the warm sun we all enjoy.

Freedom For the People
by Marcus Feng

There are no rules!
You can do whatever you want
Dr. King made freedom for the people

Dreams For All
by Alex Arrindell

He had a dream for all people
black or white
to be brothers and sisters
He had a dream for all nations and people
He sacrificed himself for us

Amazing Colorado
by Brigid Nestorick

Colorado, how amazing you are
Your sunsets are so wonderous
I can observe the Mountains from afar
The nature is magnificent
I am feeling very adventurous
Oh in the awesome Mile high
I am feeling so very courageous
Very awesome and wonderfully fun
The sun rises are very beautiful
They are enchanting as a spell
So wonderous and very colorful
Pink, yellow, red, so beautiful

Winter Stroll
by Mateo Zeiger

As I walk through the shadows
I see tracks running into the darkness of the forest ahead of me.
My feet are making a crunching sound
as I walk as loud as the birds around me.
I can feel the crisp cool air wisp past me
like a charging rhino.
My hot chocolate feels like an oven in my mouth
unlike the frosty terrain around me.
The white I see before me has a small dash of red
that belongs to the mailbox on the trail beyond.
The soft green that used to own the forest
has been grabbed by the plain white winter wonderland.
The trees loom over the tracks on the road and past the rabbit on snow.
My fingers feel so far away I can't reach them or my toes
as if they're on a string just out of my reach.

Sunny Day
by Alexander Cassel

Your voice is like the sun
It makes me want to run and have fun
In the sun.

A Goose and a Moose
by Sophia DeShazer

There once was a silly goose
Who became friends with a moose
They had lots of fun
While they like to run
And now their pants are loose

You Grow Like a Tree
by Kaylee Romero

Growing is like a tree
It happens when you hit three
My parents play ball
While I wanted to ride the rides at the mall
Laughing and crying to get my way
Then running away to go play because I got my way,
Growing is like a tree
When I feel free
trying to play ball
But I want to go to the mall
Locking myself in my room
Then leaving to look at the moon

I Am
by Lucas Apple

I am an artist and animator
I make so many drawings (that a lot like)
and make lots of animations people like.
I am a dreamer
I sleep and always dream, even when I'm resting!
I am an eater
I eat a lot and I really love to eat,
but I love family and friends way, way, way more!
I am a player
I play Battle Cats on my iPad and I play other games which are not mobile games.
I am a helper (sort of)
I do what people ask and sometimes pick up their items
and give it back to them.
I am a washer (sort of)
I sometimes put plates and utensils in the dishwasher where they go.

Love Is Better Than Hate
by Tyler Borisovskiy

Love is good
Love can beat hate
Hate should not be used.

The Beautiful World
by Nolan Gallardo

Nature's beauty sings.
Chirping birds and happy trees.
The clean water flows.
Birds fly through the sky.
The fresh air feels wonderful.
Nature gives us gifts.

Crack of the Bat!
by Hannah Fisher

CRACK!
Ball goes soaring.
Crowds cheering.
Around first I go.
CLANG!
The ball bangs off the fence.
Flying around second.
Dirt running through my cleats.
Swinging wide, leaving third in my dust.
Coaches yelling with excitement
SAFE!
On to the next crack of the bat.

Who I Am
by Gregory Floyd

I am an artist
I love to draw
I don't like painting
but I like sketching
I am an older brother
my sibling is a boy
his name is Aiden
I love him
I am funny
I like making jokes
when someone says something funny
I laugh a lot
I am smart
I love science
I try my best to complete my work

Spring
by Kaitlin Mar

Spring is very nice
A nice season is coming
Cool leaves grow in Spring.

Life
by Janelle Enu

Life can crumble.
Life can break.
Life can turn into an earthquake.
Life can be fun,
Life can have love.
Life is in your control.

Colorado
by Ava Hegarty

Camping is really great
skiing is so fun
hiking paths are beautiful
we are not quite done
The bluebird sky says, oh wow!
The weather here's great
I wish summer was here now
summer breeze, so cool
There's beautiful columbines
calming ski resorts
on our paths luscious plants
here's our tennis courts

B-Ball
by Xavier Flores

On the court I see players left and right,
one did a crossover, dang that was tight!
I see that 77 on the Mavs,
that shot was right.
Luka dish to Kyrie,
swish!
Does he miss?
Then Luka again, and again.
do I hear the net starting to Hiss?
They do it all, the other team can't keep up.
They are frozen like dolls.
All around threat?
Let's bet,
will they miss?
HISSS ...

Nature
by Evan Alonso

New seeds grow in spring-
Cherry blossoms grow on trees-
Spring is wonderful!!

Creativity
by Clara Parent

I write this with freedom
the thing is, creativity is around us
we know what we love
creativity can show creativity in what we love
creativity lives in everyone
we just need to find it

The Big Mountain
by Bridget Gilbride

I love skiing it is so much fun
My favorite place to ski is Aspen
The mountains are so fun with all the runs
Make sure your boots are securely fastened
We like to stop for lunch to get food
I am with my cousins eating candy
I got Skittles, I'm in a good mood
Helping my cousins ski is quite handy
I love skiing it is so much fun
We are going to Copper for Spring Break
Spring skiing will be fun in the sun
We will end the fun day with a milkshake

Who I Am
by Dani Clarke

I am a little sister
Destanie is 13
People say we look the same
But that is not the way I like to be seen
I am a student
I don't act up
I'm used to 3's and 4's and I usually get high scores
I am a writer
My teachers praise my creativity
And I never stand down from a writing activity
I am intelligent, independent and persistent
I try not to act incompetent
I do the best I can to get acknowledgement for the hard work that I do
So, this is who I am
Who are you?

Spring
by Ilanis Semenenko

Spring's welcome day
Great wonder lies ahead
Feel the joy of spring

Ice
by Leah Rossignol

Ice is cold, it can do a lot of things
too hot, it will melt.
Ice can do the most things in water or in the freezer.
Or maybe Antarctica will do just fine.
In the cold it is as strong as a rock,
but in the heat it is as weak as a worm.

Colorado
by Rudy Maley

The capital is Denver
It is freezing in the winter
We have very weird weather
There are lots of mining and some gold
Columbine the state flower
Aquamarine the state gemstone
August first our special day
Hunting gives us an awesome tone
The Avs won the Stanley Cup
The Broncos are not very good
The Rockies hit the ball up
We produce lots of good sports

My Fat Cat
by Victoria Landes

Oh cat,
oh cat,
lounging on my mat,
you are very fat
Oh cat,
oh cat,
you're not silly
you're not lovely
you're not enticing
you are only an angry fat cat
your claws scratch
your eyes glare
Menaceful cat, you are everywhere
Oh drat! Oh my fat cat!
Where, oh where has my fat cat gone?

I Wonder ...
by Joshua Eromon

I wonder how it feels to run in the forest ... like a deer
I wonder how it feels to get hunted for food ... like a deer.
I wonder how it feels to nibble on plants in the morning ... like a deer.
I feel funny ... maybe he is wondering how it feels to be like a man.

Shooting Star
by Sofia Conigliaro

So much depends upon a
shooting star shining in
all the night
Shooting star
Shooting star
Shine so bright in all the night

Colorful Colorado
by Mia Miceli

Skiing is the best
Our skiers are very fast
Then the big sun sets
Sun rises and fun begins
We have the lark hunting
The best of them all
Our seasons are amazing
But the best is fall
We have some redrocks
National Parks are where they are
We always have blue skies
We have a lot of nice stars

Time To Rhyme
by Daney Collins

There's this girl next door, she said she likes war.
When my brother's mad, he slams his door.
I fall on the floor everytime I have to do a chore.
I try to ignore all the bore.
I always want to eat more. I walk to the store.
My mom and I walked along the shore.
My core hurts, nor do I want to admit it.
I'm sore. I look poor.
I was up all night because of a snore; I was a score.
When we went camping, I ate a s'more.
I hopped a fence. My jacket tore.
I tried gymnastics. It didn't work out.
When I went fishing, I caught a trout
Every single pig on my farm has a snout.

Friend's House
by Diondre Rios

Thursday afternoon I went to my friend's house
And we were jumping on the trampoline and I did a sick backflip
And hurt my wrist from a brick because my second grade friend
Put a brick on the trampoline and landed on the brick I screamed in pain

Love Is In the Air
by Joseph Wood

Family smiling filled with joy
Giving gifts to everyone
Mom's favorite flowers is what we buy
Chocolate sweet chocolates in all different shapes and sizes
Thankful for this lovely day
Family smiling filled with joy -

Snowboarding
by Samuel Sherburne

Fast and fun
Never done
Let's go play in the snow
Grab your board,
you won't get bored
Come on it's time to go
Ride the lift
Do some tricks
Ride the mountain all day
Head out with your friends,
Hit rails over and over again
Snowboarding is so much fun

The Beach
by Gisela Gonzalez

The sun rises and shines bright like fire
It time for Morning
While the ocean waves crash on the shore
The frightened Sandpiper birds, run away from the waves
The leaves of Palm trees sway,
And brush against each other
Crowds of people would swarm in the summer
But in fall, few people would walk instead of having fun
As if they need a distraction from something stressful
The sun comes down, the moon rises
The ocean makes a swishing sound
The birds fly away
As one day would go by from night,
Then comes another day, at the beach

Hot Pink
by Adalynn Cote

Hot pink tastes warm,
and it looks like dragon fruit,
It smells like perfume,
It is like a big warm hug,
Hot pink is really nice and cuddly.

The Homework
by Olivia Robertson

When I was in fifth grade, homework was hard
but I still needed to do it to go do something fun like swimming
So I did my homework
When I was in fifth grade, homework was hard
So I didn't do it, I went to watch TikTok instead
But then I couldn't go swimming, but I still didn't want to do it

The Finals
by Loevan Karangwa

I first step on the court
I see the other team in a huddle
Our team's coach sets up a plan
There is ten seconds left
I will get the ball and I'll shoot
I dribbled down the court with speed
I shoot, I miss but
Thankfully my teammate got the rebound
There is five seconds, I dribble
Three times I shoot (splash)
I made it and I won finals MVP
Me and my teammates cheered

I Am Olivia
by Olivia Arrindell

I am persistent
I fell again but I get well again
I cry but I smile again
I am an artist
I spin and dance, I paint with my feet
It makes everyone laugh
I am a daughter to my parents
And a friend to a friend who will be great to the end
I am creative, my work is interactive, you can imagine two things at once
I am a helper for kids half my age,
they do a lot of crafts and eat a lot of snacks
I am unique, one and only me
I am Olivia, can't you see!

I Hate Poetry
by Maddie Baker

The poetry slam didn't want to memorize, but I am.
I couldn't figure out which one of my terrible poems
to memorize so I made this one.
Hate it, love it, I don't really care for it at all.
I am definitely going to lose, so good for me
I really, really hate poetry.

County Kerry
by Grace McCaffrey

The cool Irish breeze sends a shiver down my spine
The tweet from the birds make this country mine
The ground is singing me a lowly song
Saying how the flowing grass seems to swim along
All the people we know, going row by row
Until we see our closest friends, as we do then and again

Colorado
by Emma Kramer

Adventures keep going like biking
Gardens so lush and green
And everybody keeps on hiking
Camping is so quite serene
Orange sunrises are one in a ton
We have such a warm sun
Sunsets we surely don't have none
And too we are still not done
We have flowers such as columbines
Lovely hairstreak butterflies
And we have so many green grape vines
Never to say your good byes

Worrying Dreamer
by Alaina Ricketts

I am worrying dreamer
My fears transfer to my dreams
I wish I didn't though
I wish I could dream peacefully
I always worry, I worry every day
I worry when I go to school and when I come home
I always feel alone and unknown
I am a dreamer, I always roam through my mind
when I'm sleeping, I get to live my fantasy
It's not always like rainbows and sunshine though
It can get scary
But they're my dreams

We'll Make It!
by Emeri Halleman

We are stronger and braver to keep on pushing
Falling fast without each other
Think, hope, pray- walk in our graduation gowns
2030 is our time to figure ourselves out, stand strong together!

The Key
by Henry Foulk

Hi, hello, you over there.
Um hello do you even care?
Well, I guess you do, so here's a little clue!
A clue to life, unlocking the door to freedom and hope.
This was all a dream, but not like it seemed.

I Am
by Bridget Luong

I am an artist, I'd draw in a rush.
I'll make unique art, I'd draw with a brush.
I am a daughter. To my mom and my dad,
me being me makes them feel glad.
I'm a best friend, my friendship won't end,
We've all been best friends from start to the end.
I am a reader, I read all the time,
I'm eager to read from 1 to 99.
I am a student, I read and I write.
I learn new things up until night.
There's more to who I am, what I am, and if I'm in the light,
But whoever you are, what you are, you still shine so bright!

The Horse
by Sophie Bingham

His gaze turns up towards the sky. The leaving light. The bats that fly.
A scent that drifts upon the wind has suddenly awoken him.
Danger that is drawing near.
On dark, soft paws the creature creeps, towards the wild herd that sleeps.
The Stallion, he lifts his head, ignoring creeping thoughts of dread.
He stares into the distant dark, as if to say
"I'm far too strong. I'll protect them for far too long."
"and by the time I stop to sleep, it could be days.
It could be weeks. you, you creature, will have gone from here.
I'll wait a week. a month. a year. so beast, you would best leave this place.
Goodbye, goodbye, goodbye.
And as the light of day's dawn seeps, the mountain lion, off it creeps.
The horse can finally rest his head. His eyes drift shut.
Now off to bed.

Spring
by Ethan Zachariah

Flowers bloom
Plants grow tall
Spring is here!

I Can Do
by Karim Zineddine

I'm kind and I lost my mind saying I'm fine in little mines.
I'm an animal lover, I'm also a big brother.
I am a gamer going my hardest, I really go the farthest.
I am super fast but I'm in last in a cast.
I'm a traveler in Rome, but I got stuck in a dome.

My Amazing Goal For the Floor
by Beckett Watson

I love to jump!
I love to soar!
I love to be on the floor
I love gymnastics, it opens a door
especially on the floor
Oh sure the other events are cool
but sometimes they're a bore
The floor is never a chore
I really adore the floor
The floor is never a bore
I will practice, practice, practice until I make that goal
I know I can, I know I can, I know I can make my goal!
The Olympics are my goal to do it on the floor

Hopeless
by Lydon Cole

Sometimes you feel hopeless
Like you have nobody to rely on
Sometimes you might feel like there are sharp knives splitting your heart
Sometimes you might feel like a mountain with a never-ending avalanche
Hopeless
I saw my father laying there
Looking in his eyes made me feel so much doubt
He was right there
But it seemed like he didn't even exist
I pretended, hoping to forget this day
Hopeless
Like a city in a drought
Cancer..
His answer is always, "Courage son, Courage."

Sunsets and Beaches
by Laurel Drabek

Sunsets and beaches
They look like peaches
They smell like the sea
Luckily no leeches
Wish there were peaches
Some don't like them but they settle fine with me

When All Is Gone
by Lucy Cavelli

In this generation,
Most people are brats
And they act like the world is theirs.
Ungrateful for what they have,
Laptops, phones, TVs, and more
Some are so spoiled they're rotten to their core.
Their parents are their servants,
Bringing them everything they want.
But when their parents are gone,
Then they're slowly left to rot.
Their life is an unsolved puzzle,
That never has an end
And the puzzle will never be solved,
Until they make amends.

Axolotls
by Ian Kim

Just like you and me,
Axolotls have a home with friends and family.
They eat the fish their mother gave,
They hunt so they can live and play.
They find a mate after a long journey,
then make love and babies to expand their tree.
Floating around in a bed of pondweeds,
Axolotls take many naps to get a good night's sleep.
Baby pink and black, an axolotls' sensitive skin
Is cut by fishing nets and soaks toxins in.
Chemicals sting beady black eyes;
In dark, murky waters, no one hears their cries.
When people take lake water out,
Axolotls there face a terrible drought.
Fisherman capture them to sell their meat,
Until there will be no more axolotls left to eat.
Friends listen and care, with open hearts,
To save the axolotl, everyone needs to do their part.
Help to restore the lake's clear blue waters
So there will be homes for axolotl sons and daughters.

Air Jordans
by Ryan Cates

My friends and I
want to go to the mall
to get some of the new Air Jordan 4's
We get to the mall and it was filled with people
and little toddlers
But when we get to the shoe store all the shoes were sold out
Except for the ones we don't like

I Am
by Dean Gerard

I am a basketball player
but not a brick layer
I'm gonna be in the NBA
I can't wait for that day
I'm also a skater
and a very good educator
I'm no hater, but I'm greater
I'm a football player
and a very good delayer
My parents are my tax payers but that's ok
but every day I'm down by the bay
I'm a nice brother and a very good bluffer
but don't worry, I always recover

My Dream
by Mirei Gonzalez

My dream is to end poverty
To see smiles on every child and adult
To see that nobody is picking from the trash
To have equality and equity once and for all
My dream is to see a better earth
To see a clear ocean
To not see any garbage on the floor
To see the whole world squeaky clean
My dream is to end animal abuse
I don't want to see animals being starved or locked in a cage
Squeezed or being hit
Scratched or getting scared when they see somebody
My dream is to end segregation
To see every race treated equally
To see everybody with harmony
To find every race anywhere
My dream is to just be me
In a peaceful world
Striving with joy and glee
Hoping that one day everything is fixed

Things That I Am
by Jonathan Apple

I am a dreamer
I dream really big
But sometimes
I can just forget the simplest of things
I'm also an illustrator
But sometimes
I can't draw anything
Not only that
But I'm also a thinker
Being a thinker is something I do
What about you?

Get Back Up Again
by Lauren Straker

I am dancer turning around
and when I fell I touched the ground.
I am a female walking down the street
and someone says, "you're not like me."
You said, "Oh well, that's okay,
because I like myself anyway."
You are beautiful. And when someone says you're not,
you keep on walking down the block.
You are not perfect but you try your best
and the next time you talk you will not be depressed.

An Ode To Frida Khalo
by Fiona Osorio

So talented, so artistic.
you went through so much and lived!
You brought ART!!! To the world you are an inspiration to all.
Your differences and your strengths made you so special.
You did not care what people thought of you.
You died so young it was not fair.
It was not fair that you could not walk.
It was not fair that drivers are reckless
You are the queen of self portraits to this day.
You painted your pain in your beautiful art.
You are beautiful and inspire all artists in the world.
Probably the most famous
Probably the most hard working
You're probably the most famous because of your unique personality
and your multifaceted life.
You did not smile.
You lived in the Casa Azul from birth to death.
Your beautiful house

How We Are Special
by Adam Badal

I'm special and you are too!
All of us are smart, some need more time
Some of us like play, some of us like to work
But no matter what, we are all different
We love to have fun
We like to relax
We do what we like
Some are good at math
Some are good at art and some are good at ELA
But we are together special

My Reflection
by Kristina Asriyants

As I look in the mirror, all I can see,
A beautiful girl, looking right back at me.
The reflection is pretty, for all I can see.
And guess what? That reflection is me!
I am a daughter, grand-daughter, great-grand-daughter too
I am a student, a good one indeed.
Big, fat books, are the ones that I read.
I am a sister, a friend, a creator
I am a poet, an artist, a bracelet maker
I am a singer, I write some songs too,
I am amazing! How about you?

Formula One Racing
by Phoebe Douglas

F is for faster-than-fast.
O is for "only some can win",
R is for races all over the globe.
M is for Monza, Monaco, and Miami.
U is for unexpected occurrences.
L is is for losing the rear sometimes.
A is for awesome, 2-time-champ, number ...

1, Max Verstappen.

R, racing is quite fun.
A, Azerbaijan, Austin, and Australia.
C, checkered flags at the end.
I, Imola, Italy unfortunately canceled.
N, Nurburgring, Netherlands.
G, Go Max Verstappen!!!

This poem will help you learn about F1 in a whiz,
and I hope you understand how outstanding it is.

The New Kitten
by Jayden Nelson

I was approaching my house
I was shocked with what I saw
I saw a cute baby kitten on the couch
And he had one of the cutest paws
He was tired at daylight
And hyper at nighttime
He slept by me at light
And at night he had the best time

Snowy Forest
by Alyana Venzor

On a snowy afternoon,
An arctic fox was walking through the woods.
He was walking for hours to look for food.
Then he saw a deer on the ground
Because a tree branch fell on him.
When the deer was walking,
The fox wanted to eat him
But then he had this sensation
That the fox wanted to help him.
It was weird.
He had a bad reputation.
He was confused but he helped the deer.
He asked if the deer knew the feeling
And he said, "It was kindness"

The Astounding Beginning
by Elana Choi

She then explained my dreadful fate.
I could imagine her taking my heart
and breaking it with her bare hands as she said that.
In a blink of an eye, I turned the opposite way and sprinted home.
With an emerging waterfall in my eyes,
I felt the irresistible impulsive urge to rip my heart out of my chest.
I desired no use of it anyway.
Time flew until right before my eyes was the burgundy red door to my house.
My hand looked as if it had absolutely no business in staying still
and calm as I unlocked the door.
After furiously taking my shoes off,
I ran to my room faster than any car could drive.
I rushed inside and used all my might to slam my bedroom door shut.
I then slumped down on the floor and let my tears run.
They kept flowing to the point I was running out of tissues for them.
Then right out of the blue, I looked up as my sweet hazel eyes turned devilish red.
I no longer wore my heart on my sleeve.
I was willing to dedicate my life to prove her wrong, and I swore to do exactly that

I Am
by Kaylee Flores

I am an artist
paints and pastels
all over while
I'm painting a Range Rover
I am a reader
I love to be a reader
reading scary stories
while also reading shorties
I am a sis
giving my sister a goodnight kiss

Beautiful Colorado
by Katherine Gaines

Smell the flowers, see the bees,
hear the wind rustle through the trees.
Come see the mountains, cause we have a lot,
care for a picnic? we have just the right spot.
We are known for our beautiful skies, in Colorado no one cries.
Everyone's happy all day long, in Colorado nothing goes wrong.
When people come, they never want to leave,
all of our goals we proudly achieve.
come to Colorado, and please don't be late,
because our Colorado is the best state.

Nature and Animals
by Yonah Shimborsky

The plants, the trees, the hard working bees,
Even the cows make a food called cheese.
But sometimes you see something, you might want to freeze,
But take a look around, smell some flowers (you might sneeze!).
Hippos and rhinos got the biggest toes,
But elephants have the biggest nose!
There are even some plants,
That could scare you out of your pants!
They eat pesky things, like flies and gnats,
This plant is called the Venus fly trap- don't touch its hairs, or it will go snap!!!
Tigers and lions and pumas and more,
Just look around and see what's in store.
Dragonflies can seem like terrible pests,
But at catching mosquitoes they are the best!
The Sequoia tree is so very tall,
Be careful, you don't want it to fall!
Leaf cutter ants eat lots of plants,
Don't let them crawl up your pants!
So thank you animals, trees and plants,
You really make me want to dance!

Basketball Wows & Woes
by Ashlyn Lemieux

I dribble,
I shoot, it hits the board.
I dribble, I shoot, oh look! I've scored!
My friends, my family and I,
watch as the ball soars through the sky.
It's in the net, oh I might cry.
The game is over, it is done!
For the first time ever, my team has won!
The Bucks beat the Bulls,
And it was fun.
But for me, my basketball career has just begun.

Hope
by Freya Smith

A single dove
Swoops in and out
Through trees filled
With a bright orange glow
The creatures look up
A small spark of hope
Drifts to their hearts
Like a tiny lantern.
They crowd together
And start their journey
Following the fortunate flying dove.
Thousands of dark ashes plummet
But all are oblivious.
Even when there is chaos
There is still hope.

Looking Forward To Spring
by Antonio Albano

Looking forward to spring
Thinking of all the fun that it will bring
The weather will start to get nice
The sun will melt away any ice
I can go outside and ride my bike
And play all the sports that I like
I can play baseball with my team
I can layout outside, take a nap and have a dream
I will try to see the Easter bunny
And hang out with my friends that are funny
I can swim in my pool
We are getting closer to the end of school
Before you know it, it will be summer
Spring will be over, what a bummer

I Am
by Joshua Rivera

I am me
I love to be
I love to be me
I am a reader
I fly through books like a jet
I am a basketball player
I shoot hoops and they fly through
like a pack of birds
I am a big brother
I am a great hugger

Birthday Plan
by Annabelle Lermond

It's my birthday
What should I do?
Go swimming?
Go to the zoo?
I don't know what I,
Should do.
What about a
Trampoline park?
That should be fun.
It will be more fun than,
A fun run.
So that's it.
That's what we will do.
Scratch the swimming.
Scratch the zoo.

Maui Pools
by Ava Calhoun

The cool water flows
The sound of palm trees blow
The rain starts to fall
The hot tub steams
The kids smile with glee
They all feel free
Pineapples are ripe
It all feels right
The scent of sunscreen lifts to the sky
Tiki torches say good-bye
It's not as hot
While all slides stop
No more sun
Day is done
Everybody knows all pools are closed

She Had Some Dogs
by Nalini Claveau

She had some dogs who were glass and would break.
She had some dogs who were paper and would fly away in the wind.
She had some with fur and teeth.
She had some dogs who were movies and drama.
She had some dogs that would walk and run.
She loved her dogs.

Dreams
by Alexander Cantwell

Dreams become imagination
They become creativity
From aliens to dinosaurs, they all come to life
Imagination never stops; goes on for infinity.
Dreams become imagination
Dreams are wonderful.
They give us curiosity and hope.
They make us wonder about our future like a butterfly
and the past like a caterpillar.
Dreams are wonderful.
Dreams give hope and curiosity
Dreams are dreams
Turn the darkness into light.
Dreams are everything

I Am Me
by Brandon Lax

I am creative
Thinking about everything
Making about everything
Saying about everything
I am smart
getting 100 every day
getting 100 every night
100, 100
I am athletic
playing basketball
playing baseball
playing football
playing every sport you know
I am a brother
Just asked my brother
He said "Heck yea you're my brother"
So I'm a brother
I am a gamer
playing *Call of Duty* cause that's my duty
playing *Fortnite* because it's *Fortnite*

Business Man
by Julian Perez Lopez

I want to be a business man
It will take 30 years
work hard, study well, never give up, go to school
I will study, study, study
to earn some money
my business will fly, fly so high, high
I will make some money for my family
so I will work, work hard that is my goal

My Brother
by Laina Stauch

The brother of my life is dead and not alive.
He is the one that is kind.
He will make me cry.
I am sad of the madness
He is in Heaven where you can't tell him what's wrong
I want him in my house,
And I wish my brother was here with me.
He died that day on January twenty-seven.
Someday you will find your love again.
They will always be in your life,
They will always be in your love and family.
My brother is happy now.

The Quiet Bird
by Ella Seidlitz

As the quiet bird sits
On the dark wooden post,
The rumor has been heard
I am the quiet bird.
I sit and listen
To the teacher talk,
Then I remember
I am the quiet bird.
The bird shares its trill
As it sits on the hill.
The rumor has been heard
I am the quiet bird.
After the shadows I see at night
I struggle to escape the fright,
With each rumor told,
Everyone knows I am the quiet bird.
I sit and listen
To the teacher talk,
Then I remember
I am the quiet bird, I am the quiet bird.

Spring
by Vivian Cho

I plop down on the fresh grass,
with the spring break that just passed.
Beautiful flowers bloom,
while my mom cleans my room.
Butterflies flutter through the sky,
while the bees pass by.
Sneezing and coughing, rubbing my red eyes,
in the night I see the moon rise.

The Summer
by Karis Holtz

The sun is so light,
And the clouds so bright.
I love the sky,
I wish I could fly.
The puppies are happy,
And they are nappy.
I will lie in the grass,
Watching the clouds pass.
I will hum a tune,
While the flowers bloom.
I watch the pond,
While I praise God.

22 a Poem
by Greyson Fries

I see a small number outside my window.
22, 22
I've seen this number day and night
goodness, goodness gracious.
22, 22
was my number in class
the 4th grade number I sit here at last,
I've see it all day and all night.
22, 22
well that ain't a freight
my dad's favorite number,
and finally it's night
22, 22
I'm her finally at last
I see it at football games, car shows, and races.
I see this number day and night
all day and night.
22, 22
What a spectacular sight
I see 22 all day and all night

My Dog Pip
by Adrianna Kampfer

There once was a dog
whose name was Pip.
He died from being old.
Oh little poor Pip!
He was really cute.
He was a protective dog.
Oh little Pip,
I love you so much!

Wishes
by Liam Jones

Do you have a job?
Yes, I have a dog!
I said job!!
I'm not a blob!!
I said job not blob!!
My name isn't Rob!!
I said job not Rob!!
I am not a slob!!
Do you have a job!!
I'm not a snob!!
Do you have a job!!
I'm not a nob!!

The Fuzzy Worm
by Lailee Myron

The fuzzy worm
He liked to squirm
He liked to play
All through the day
He tried to fly
About the sky
But he fell
So he said "oh well"
He floated up like a balloon
And made a cocoon
Then it twitched
And it glitched
Out he came
Like a burning flame
Finally he could fly
So high in the sky
Off the ground
He finally found
his brothers
And the others.

My Harness
by Scarlett Jablonski

harness, harness,
i see it on the shelf
even though no one knows
it is my greatest strength,
and weakness,
my harness gives me hope

Real Friends
by Madison Poublon

Friends will always be there,
Even if gloom is in the air.
Friends will cheer you up,
Even if you are stuck with no luck.
Friends are honest.
They will never break a promise.
That's what a real friend is.

I Am Very Special
by Evan Dent

I am generous person, spreading kindness along the way,
matter of fact I show it every day.
I'm a thoughtful person, thinking of other people before myself,
I love giving to everyone else.
I am a basketball player, dominant on the court.
Basketball is my favorite sport!
I'm smart, even good thinking in the dark!
I'm a learner, making sure to learn new things every day
I'm always taking in everything my teachers say!
I'm very special in many ways
I hope you say that to yourself every single day!

Nature Is Powerful
by Elizabeth Stead

Nature is wild like wildflowers
It is beautiful and abundant with animals, trees and space
Even a weed looks majestic in nature
Can you imagine?
Instead of going on devices, go outside and play
Be with plants and animals, and let yourself be free
Imagine
Discover
Plant flowers in the sunshine and dance in the rain
People will find joy, love and confidence ...
You just have to go outside
Nature is powerful

Starlight
by Ava Friday

Starlight,
You shine so blindingly bright,
You really are a wonderful sight,
When your light wraps around me tight,
I can see you ignite in the fright of the night ...
Can you see me Starlight?

Basketball
by Brock Wittler

The smooth court,
The shoes on my feet,
The swish of the net,
The crowd screaming,
The dribble of the ball,
The cameras watching,
It's Basketball season!

How Many Times?
by Chloe Blomquist

How many times will I try?
How many times will I cry?
How many times will I say "goodbye?"
How many times will I fly?
How many times will I be shy?
How many times will I put it so high?
How many times will it go dry?
How many times will I reply?
How many times will it die?
How long will it take me to make up my mind?
Thank you for helping me try.

Animal Shelter
by Danica Ghezzi

I want to be a person
who works for the animal shelter
to care for the animals.
I love animals.
I will train them to sit, stay, paw, down.
I love animals.
Make sure they are healthy,
Keep them safe, feed them.
I will make sure they have a home.
Even though it might be smelly, welly
I will play with them
I love animals.

My Roof Was Actually Leaking
by Malina Peters

Roses are red
My roof is leaking
JJ came for
housekeeping

Homes
by Archer Williams

Our homes; as we march forward to being adults.
Our homes, loving homes, caring homes.
We leave the sure chance that our friends, who are family, will stay
We must have confidence and courage to brave this world and life
People find their secure position on Earth
Creating permanent homes, houses.
We use our knowledge to stumble through life, an imperfection
But till 2030, I don't leave my nest, I have homes

Fall
by Kaitlyn Figgs

Leaves dancing to the ground,
Hardly ever making a sound
They cover the ground like a sheet,
And crunch under my feet
A sweet-smelling pumpkin pie,
Whipped cream is all I need to apply
Fluffy mashed potatoes with gravy on top,
Cranberry sauce flowing down the turkey just won't stop
The temperature is slowly dropping,
The hot weather is now stopping
A nice fall breeze swirls around me,
Snuggling up in a blanket with hot chocolate is the key

All About My Dream Space
by Benjamin Manzo

I always wanted to be in space. I sometimes shine, sometimes not.
But why am I sometimes shiny, sometimes dark.
What's happening. I'm so confused.
The first person to be on different land was Neil Armstrong.
I want to be like him but instead of being on the moon I want to be first on Mars.
I was born on Jupiter, never Earth.
We aliens can contact Earth but I'm still a kid so I can't.
I will soon be in a place with no huge deadline storm, and where it's warm.
I want to see how it feels off my planet, Jupiter.
Ahh! Oh it was all a dream.
It would be fun, now I wonder should I go to space or not?

Cherry Blossom
by Rio Skye Abizeid

Pink cherry blossoms -
Falling from the big brown trees -
Beautiful flowers

I Am Me!
by Brianna Cherny

I am brave going on speedy roller coasters
I am shining like a shooting star
I am a gymnast doing flips and tricks
I'm a powerful brave Taurus
I am an artist, making masterpieces all the time like I'm doing right now!
I'm a great, caring family member and friend to all!
I'm funny like a bunny
That's who I am!

Artist!
by Anna Bostick

Do I see you, do I not?
You see my mind while in your cot.
What do you keep, what do you treasure?
Paint and pens I love beyond measure.
What skills do you need, where did you learn them?
I'm talented in lead and pencil. I got these skills at SAIC.
With whom do you work with, where do you work?
With all my friends and in the studio.
What do you have, where did you get it?
I have love from my family
What can you be, oh what can be you?
I am an artist, can't you see

Summer Vacation In Italy
by Kendra Gamberini

Italy
Something you see during summer vacation in Italy:
historical sites in: Naples, Rome, Florence, Venice, Milan
Something you hear during summer vacation in Italy:
People speaking in Italian, lots of Italian
Something you smell during summer vacation in Italy:
Delicious puff pastries and the famous food, like pasta, pizza,
spaghetti, lasagna, risotto and the seafood.
Something you taste during summer vacation in Italy:
Every delicious thing there is to taste
Something you feel during summer vacation in Italy
Excited

Hockey Or Football
by Treven Maytum

I'm gonna start football soon
I play hockey too
I don't know what is better
I like football and hockey
But nevermind
I don't know what is better
Hockey is on ice which is cool
But in football you can tackle
I don't know what is better
Football you throw with a ball
Hockey you pass with a stick
Nevermind, I know what's better

Poe
by Jace Beaver

Poe, my beloved Labrador, Poe
Poe, the fluffiest lab, danced in snow
Poe, named after the famous Edger Alan Poe
Poe, had a birthmark, a raven, we loved him so
Poe, had died of cancer, I loved him with my heart
I love him so much, I made him art.
Oh! Poe I love thee so
I missed how ye danced in snow
Glitch would love you,
just as I do.
Rest in peace,
my dearest friend.
The End

Fennec Fox!
by Helen Brain

Hello again ...
Nice to see you ...
I love you.
You're so cute.
Cause I love you!
Adorable I say!
What if we meet today!
Thank you, say hoo!
Oh I love you ...
Oh yes I do ...
It was just nice to have you.
Oh you're so cute ... I'll just miss you.
So it's time to say goodbye ...
But I will always love you!

Who I Am
by Darla Passanisi

I am a gamer
I am an artist
I am a hard worker
I am a cooker
I am a reader
I am smart
I am sweet and very nice
I am friendly
I am grateful
I am sometimes crazy
I am noisy
I am funny
I am a learner

Yellow
by Oakley Doman

Yellow
Yellow is Sunflower
Yellow is summer
Yellow is the color of happiness
Yellow is Hawaii sand
It smells like lemons
It tastes like lemonade
It sounds like splashes
It looks like the sunshine
Yellow feels like heat
Yellow makes me want to swim
Yellow is vacation

Baseball
by Marik Esselink

The pitch is thrown,
while the ball gets blown,
the carack of the bat,
makes the fans lift their hat.
The ball flies so high,
as it soars through the sky,
the power of the ball,
puts it over the wall.
It's a home run,
and the crowd thinks it's fun,
the noise of the crowd,
makes the stadium loud.
The fans had big fun,
too bad the game is now done.

The Warmth!
by Justice Jackson

I love the crispness of the hot, shiny sun in the spring
and the sand in my burnt toes.
I love the way the cool water lets me feel alive and well
after tanning in the scorching sun.
I love the warmth!

Space!
by Ryan Hollander

I am more than you can ever imagine.
When you look up at the sky there I am.
I will always be there, longer than anyone or anything.
I am more awesome than you can ever imagine.
I am space!

Growing Up
by Niko Carrasco

Young
To old
Good memories
Bad ones too,
It was nice being you
Now I'm older
And I am almost older
Than dinosaurs
Just kidding I would be
DEAD.

A Wonderful Winter
by Christian Ludwig

Snow is falling quite low, there is a sound you may hear coming rather near.
It is a crowd, shouting rather loud, up on a hill, getting a thrill.
All sitting on sleds, having fun with their friends.
You can build a snowman, put a tree in a van, and decorate the tree for all to see.
Happy people are singing, and bells are ringing
and Santa will bring children new toys, each bringing twice as much joy.
Reindeer on roofs clacking their hoofs, getting ready to fly, oh so high.
In the town square there is a light, coming from a tree, oh so bright.
Carolers singing "O Holy Night", oh what a beautiful sight.
You could see the sleds, fast as lightning;
Riders holding on with hands cold as ice, all while a mother shouts
"Oh please play nice!"
Then you can walk inside and begin to warm up.
You can sip some hot chocolate warm as -
Ouch! I just burnt my tongue!

I Am Me
by Abby Apergis

I am a friend, I am a sister, I am me.
I am smart, I am a student, I am me.
I am nice, I am sweet, I am polite, I am me.
I like movies, I like shows, this is me.
Let me see, well I am me.
I am a friend, I am with you till the end.

You Can Make a Difference
by Jayden Alison

making a difference isn't that hard
and it doesn't matter who you are
It doesn't matter where you are from or what you look like
or what you wear you can make a difference anywhere.
at the store, maybe even at the park, you can make a spark in someone's heart.
be kind and be nice and know that you are making a difference.

The Birthday Plan
by Isabella Hennard

I love Jojo Siwa, her songs are loved
so for my birthday I made a list
I want balloons that float high
the concert of a lifetime
friends to sing with me and her
a huge Jojo Siwa cake
all the fruits I want
take a nice picture with Jojo
and see her dog Bow Bow
Oh how fun will that be
for Jojo Siwa to see me

Song of the Sapling
by Islay Blackburn

Tree, Tree, so young and bold, how do you stretch your limbs so?
You strain and pull through canopy's hole to await the daybreak sun.
Tree, Tree, so tall and strong, sure and calm,
how do you hold yourself still, so still?
A snail's trail, a snake's tale, told in the tree's calm voice.
Sing, sing, oh tree, with the rush, gush, swish, hush.
Nothing will ever scare you, oh will they dare you,
tree so tall and strong, young in your song.
Tree, tree, so small and calm, how do you grow your buds so?
Green, then yellow, red, orange.
Don't you feel rushed in such pretty colors around you?
You are truly beautiful, your work was fruit-i-ful.

The Kind Love
by Zoey Lindor

The day of love is a happy long fun.
While we get cards they are having fun playing along.
The wind is going heavy as we think of the dearest we love.
The gifts we get are a symbol of love.
Being with them is a moment of love.

Power
by Naftali Rubinson

Everyone has a power-
Some are good at sports-
Some are very flexible and some can stable animals and more.
Some can play the trumpet, some can play guitar
and some can be creative and make some out of tar.
No matter what your power is it's something good-
as long as you use it as you should.

Shooting Star
by Claire Ma

The Galaxy shines upon the drawn stars,
O'er the Moon, lays a tune singing and bringing hope.
Fly,
Fly,
Away, into the crystal Moon,
The children watching, and waiting,
To see it come again.
The stars draining' the light,
Till it's gone.
Glowing silently upon the earth.
Shooting stars ...
Shooting stars ...

I Had Some Pugs
by Sophie Adkins

I had some pugs that were bossier than their parents.
I had some pugs that were poorer than pencils.
I had some pugs that were cheerful as cheerleaders.
I had some pugs that were neater than desks.
I had some pugs that were more athletic than the Mona Lisa.
I had some pugs that were honesty and beauty.
I had some pugs that were lazier than a bag of chips.
I had some pugs that were artistic with Minecraft.
I had some pugs that were more horrible than ever but they don't care.
I had some pugs that were mean but nice.
I love my pugs.

Summer
by Caroline Land

Sunny
Umbrella
Making new friends
More rain
Eating Ice cream
Reading

I Like To Draw
by Sareen Brar

I like to draw,
Lots of colors I saw,
I hope my cat's paw,
She scratched with her claw,
I eat meat that's raw,
I like to draw!

Time
by Nora Petersen

It ticks.
It tocks.
There's never enough.
There's always too much.
The pendulum swings back and forth
Back and forth
Back and forth.
Time flies like a soaring bird.
Time is as quiet as a whisper unheard.
When you go to sleep
Time doesn't make a single peep.

This Is Who I Am
by Leah Goldshmidt

I'm a gymnast who flips, splits
and spins through the air
it feels like I'm in a different universe
when I am there.
I know I'm a tennis player
that tries hard enough to succeed.
I jump and run so everyone can see.
If I lose I'll try to win next time
The actress I am flows through the air
I act and jump-spins in the flowing wind that I see
I'm a daughter from my mother,
we play, watch, and always do something together and forever.

I Hear My School Singing
by Lexi Einspahr

I hear ... balls bouncing bing bong
I hear ... computers typing click clack
I hear ... the teachers teaching yak, yak
I hear ... pencils, pens and markers writing scritch scratch
I hear ... kids yelling at recess "Tag, you're it!"
I hear ... kids talking at lunch "Blah Blah"
I hear my school singing

Stars
by Sylvie Gagnon

Stars
Millions of shining lights spread across the dark blue sky
Stars
Each and every one is special in their own way
Stars
Each star is like a person.
Every one of them have a different Meaning. Purpose. Direction in the sky.

The Dreadful Days
by Olivia Wong

I see kids lying
I see kids crying
I see kids whining
I see kids denying others
I see kids drying ripped clothes
I see kids eyeing each like they're going to have a hard fight
I see kids pieing others that are not supposed to be treated that way

My Wish For the World
by Owen Niznik

If the world was my wish, it would be
Clean
If the world was my dream, it would be
Peaceful
If the world was my heart, it would be
Kind
If the world was me, it would be
Covered in trees
But it's not.
The world has litter,
The world has war,
The world has bullies,
The world has few trees
What is the world supposed to be?

Happy Things
by Sophia Ruberto

I am sweet
I an nice
I help people
do things right
I am kind
like wine

Soccer
by Laura Magenheimer

Soccer
Fun and enjoyable
Running freely
As great as chocolate, but greater
If only the weather was better

My Future Life
by Stella Melby

I'm seeing skiing in my future
I love, love skiing.
It is fun
to be on the run.
I fly fast
I never get last
If I'm flying fast.
I flew down the blue
to get to the double black.
Swish, swish, swish
I wish, wish, wish
to see skiing in the future.

Gotta Catch em' All
by Damien Baker

Gotta catch 'em all
Better not let 'em fall
As we throw the pokéballs
The Pokémon starts a ball
Look, I found a Raichu
He made me say Achoo!
When I sneeze he scatters
I go to see what matters
I'm surprised to see a Raichu family
What am I doing? Have I lost my sanity?
Pokémon aren't real
I'm being such an eel!

The Wonderful World
by Craig Adragna

The world is so wonderful
It is very colorful
Sometimes it gets crazy-
also lazy
But it's just so wonderful

Lightning McQueen Sees a Cow
by Zaco Frihauf

Lightning McQueen sees a cow, ow
Then he goes Kachow, ow
He's a speed racer
Even though he looks like my eraser
Kachow

There Was a Leprechaun With One Shoe
by Yazlin Cabrera

There was a leprechaun with one shoe
Who had lots to do
Its work was so hard
That he acted like a dart
But could never get through

Serene
by Jordan Thompson

Crowds of people
yelling
alone
Chaotic
Bitter
Broken
The bees are buzzing
The birds are singing
The flowers are glowing
The summer breeze is gentle
The world is serene
I am at peace

Popsicles
by Willow Hall

Popsicles are kind of cold
the flavors, oh they are bold
Popsicles, they melt
they get all over my belt
Oh, it tastes like gold

There Was a Boy Named Sue
by Roman Skazko

There was a boy named Sue
That liked to wear blue
His family was glad
that he was very bad,
Because Sue liked to go to the zoo

Fast Running River
by Ryder Mathews

My time with each parent is like a fast running river
as I go back and forth like a swing hung from a tree
as I imagine I'm soaring through the thick clouds
with wind streaming through my luscious hair
and me falling from the sky into my parent's arms.

Lightning and Thunder
by Ella Eagles

BOOM,
CRASH,
There goes
The lightning
1, 2, 3, 4, 5,
High thunder
In the sky,
BOOM, BOOM, BOOM,
Woosh - a gust of wind,
Power out,
Darkness in the room,
Silence ...

3rd Place

Siena Chen

The Garden of Beauty
by Siena Chen

Summer brings big, round grapes, wholesome and sweet
The weather is warm, the sun is shining bright
Until the air turns cooler, and fall comes
The trees are almost bare
As hazel and crimson leaves slowly fall to the ground,
and a gentle, swift breeze brushes past
spreading the spirit of Autumn wherever it goes.
When fall ends
Winter takes its place
Leaving patches of snow where the leaves had fallen
A fluffy, white cover over the ground.
As the snow melts
The spring rains arrive,
a soft relaxing sound that lets you know
The flowers are brilliantly blooming.
The sun's bright rays finally shine
on the fresh red, pink, and white roses.
Nature is simply a garden of beauty.

2nd Place

Cora Seed

Hope
by Cora Seed

Hope is a powerful thing,
sometimes so subtle we can't tell it's there.
Hope is a flashlight in the dark,
a smile through anger.
It can be a feeling so strong it hurts,
But sometimes it's just
a hug after a bad day
rain after a drought
acing a test or finishing the last lap.
Maybe it's laughing after grieving,
or the doctor saying you'll be OK.
It's that little hint of light,
no matter how small, it's there.
Because a fire starts from a tiny flame,
growing and shrinking but never dying.
Hope is in every smile and laugh
in the blood and sweat and tears we shed.
Hope is EVERYWHERE,
you just have to ignite the flame.

1st Place

Graylin Khalsa-Bryant

Graylin wrote to us while in the fourth grade,
and wins $100 for the poem, "Taro."
A very relatable work,
portraying the frustrating and, at times,
helpless feeling of not being heard.
Congratulations, Graylin!

Taro
by Graylin Khalsa-Bryant

I wake from my midmorning nap
To see my favorite spot in ruin
The tree in the front yard is at an odd angle
These large metal beasts
With large sharp teeth
One of them is mauling the cherry tree
I tried to stop them by meowing
But no one listens to me
Alas, I cannot save my spot
I cry out,
But no one listens

Division II

Grades
6-7

Clandestine
by Fiona Peras

Dangers, in hiding.
The shadows are what they like,
Hidden from all life.

The World
by Raania Arif

If you can dream with no sleep
If you can think with no thought
If you can say without speaking
And try without trying
If you could be the bigger person
And not stoop so low
If you can rely and trust
If you can cry with no emotion
And jump with no excitement
If you can do then try
If you cannot then try
And if you can keep going
You are already there

The Dangers of the Sea
by Keanah Proctor

I looked at the sea from my house
and I saw a whale
It looked like a mouse
from where I was but, oh well.
At night I was a glimmer of light
A boat drifting close
And I screamed with all my might
"Please do not take my nose."
I do not know why I said that
But really, I was mixed in the confusion
To be exact
And life was really an illusion
I looked around
For something, but what?
Maybe if drowned
I would not have been cut.
I only drowned because I did not like the beach
And when I sat on the sand the waves took me
And only two searches each
Could have guaranteed
But they found me instead
And I was saved
But that was unsaid
When I could have been enslaved.

World War Two
by Landon Hall

World
Of
Radical tyrants will
Lead their
DOOM for their countries
War is just
As
Radical as the devil
The
War
Of freedom

People
by Macy Greene

So many different kinds of people
different cultures, skin colors and religions
everyone is different
everyone has something different about them
no matter what, everyone is beautiful in their own way
no matter where you come from
you are beautiful
everyone loves when you are yourself
so be yourself
and people will love you

Rain
by Eleanor Dutkiewicz

Drip, drip, drip
Raindrops land on my nose
Grey clouds as far as the eye can see
A warm smell of rain
My feet hit the rocky ground
Drops gently touch my hair
I look up at the sky
As the wind takes
The water away
Flowers tiptoeing upward
Rivers shiny with water
Boom!
Clouds crash high above
Rain falls harder
Breaking the ground
Drip, drip, drip
A passage to the sky is cleared
Rain slowly dances down
Peace is fulfilled.

Why?
by Jordan Fuller

Why do soldiers listen to the sounds of bombshells?
Why do people place burdens on trains?
Why do people help each other out?
Why do people strain their muscles?
Why do people step out of their comfort zones?
Why do people spend hours sitting at a desk?
Why do people face their fears?
Why do people ask "Why?" when they can go out and "Do."

6 Ft Hole
by Minteamir Amaral

I dug a six foot hole in the ground.
I dug and I dug and I dug until I realized I had buried myself inside.
One scoop from a shovel is equal to one mistake I have made.
Pretty soon that number grows and boom here we are. In a hole.
Made from the mistakes of my past.
The question I keep asking myself is how did you get here?
What caused you to keep making mistakes?
What caused you to not take action?
What stopped you from realizing what you've done?
Why couldn't you have noticed sooner? Why does being second suck so bad?
Why is it when I try to do something my voice, my princess,
my essence is drowned out from the person at first.
From the person that gets everything.
From the person I want to look up to but can't because my jealousy blinds me.
How can I look in a mirror every day and say I know that girl!
I know exactly who she is.
But when I go to bed every night I wonder who am I really?
We don't know who we are truly. No one does.
They may think that they do but they don't.
We all know that to some extent. And for that I don't know.
You keep asking what comes next.
What are you gonna do to take action and responsibility?
I don't know and that's the truth. Keep asking go ahead my answer
remains the same and it will until I can get myself together
and throw myself forward because I am trapped in this hole.
The rabbit hole that turned me into a person I don't want to be a person
that I am not proud of. A person that when they make one mistake
it is all over. When you make a mistake it is your funeral
and nobody comes to say nice things about you because you shut everyone out
because they tell you to figure it out but you don't know what to do.
This endless loop. Get up, go to school, have a crappy day
because of one mistake, go home scared because you know what is waiting
for you; an angry mom who asks why has nothing changed
an angry mom that says I don't know what to do with you.
But she isn't angry. Not really. Just worried about you.

Pressure To Be Perfect
by Selin Canbaz

Can't be too pretty
Can't speak my mind
Be like the others and you'll be fine
Can't make a mistake
Can't step out of line
The lines smaller and smaller
Be perfectly perfect
No flaws allowed
I've grown to know it
The pressure to be perfect
Behind the smile
The pressure is growing
The dimming light
How long till I can't take it
How long till the bridge breaks
How long till the dam floods
How long till I can't take the pressure of perfection

Her Thorns Surround Me
by Aranza Yamileth Aguirre Reyna

This cold and cruel world leaves a bitter taste on my tongue.
The misdeeds of others in the end are the lashes that hit my back,
although I'm tough it's not enough.
I could reach for the stars all night long, till the birds sing their sweet song.
Yet it will all be in vain for others to are gain.
Once a beautiful flower she has now wilted bent by the wind and rain.
In a distant past it was a spark lit aflame but now she's burnt out,
only ashes remain. My pleading cries for help are muffled by the water
slowly entering my lungs, "pull me out!" I scream, the rain; my tears
are now the only thing I can hold near and dear. But still I drone on and on,
straight lines, keep it neat for that's the only thing keeping you from falling down
that hole left in your heart. The alcohol and drugs have ruined them
and so much more, you don't want that you could be left alone on the shore
left to rot and die, despite all this, he's my sweet escape, while he still brings me
pain, it's an addicting rush that makes my heart bleed onto the thorns of lust,
or is it just me? Am I the one wrapping my thorns around her heart
keeping a horrible fear in the dark? For I find myself hiding away from her,
my greatest fear in the end is me. She's afraid and hides from love,
afterall, if she can't find the strength to love herself, how could she love him?
This rose was never meant to last. She's the one with tainted hands,
her reddened tears have engraved my skin. I hate her, that weed!
But she and I are one in the same and only I can break these earthly chains,
I'm responsible for all these tears and pain. I'm tired, I can't do it anymore,
she masks herself through perfection to hide those scars.
When I take my last breath on this cold, wretched ground, in this cold desolate
place she'll be the only one around and maybe then she'll learn how to love.

By the Seaside
by Max Kjeldsen

By the seaside,
Where the crabs reside
Along with the smooth black oysters and the miniature clams that burrow
On the bubbling foamy shore.
Or farther out
With the sandpapery gray sharks
And the schools upon schools of fish,
The fishermen working hard above them.
The wind blows
Carrying the coolness of the cerulean sea,
All the way to the land
On those shores
With the children wading in the water
Far from the talented surfers riding waves
And the burnt beach bums lazing around
On a warm summer day
And as the people pack up and leave
And the fisherman heads back to port,
The moon shines on the water for few to see,
A marvelous sight in the cool ocean breeze.

What If I Ate That Ice Cream
by Olivia Bratton

Almost a year ago, my grandma and I got into a Car accident.
We had just had lunch, and my grandma got an Ice cream cone.
She asked me if I could finish it for her, I said "No, I'm too full" So we left.
Just then the accident happened, The sound of tires screeching, Loud crash!
The sight of my grandma's frighten face, Hair over my eye's,
The thought of "I'm I dying?"
No one should have those thoughts.
I sat on the wet, wet grass Having one thought cross my mind.
"What if I ate that ice cream?"
If I ate that ice cream, none of this would have happened.
If I ate that ice cream, I would have been able to go home.
If I ate that ice cream, I would have had a sleepover with my best friend.
If I ate that ice cream, I wouldn't have to witness
my grandma breaking down in front of me,
My hero, my wonder woman, breaking down to tears in front of me.
If I ate that ice cream, I would be okay…
So fella's, gall's, non-binary pals, I leave you at this.
Next time you or someone you know are driving recklessly…
Think of the person on the other side of the road,
Is a life you are putting in jeopardy.
And after all that happened, that person will leave with one question
on their mind, "What if…" And for me…
What if I ate the ice cream.

Misunderstood
by Parker Johnson

When I'm losing friends and life is sad.
And the sky above is dreary.
I can count on video games to make me glad.
I win a game and I'm very cheery.
But when I lose a game I become mad.
I freak out in a storm of anger.
And suddenly this game was bad.
My mood drops like an anchor.
My parents come home and see my rage
My father said:
"Son, you're not acting your age!"
He simply shakes his head.
My anger became a cage.
He sent me to my bed.
He gave me a page.
To write where my actions led.
Dear Father, I apologize.
But stuff has happened at school.
It's important that you sympathize.
What happened was very cruel.
I came home very emotional.
And went straight to my games.
I know I got quite commotional.
But I vented all the same.

Nonsense
by Enzo Carpio

Fish, fish, fish, 3 fish next fish five fish, seven fish, what great fish.
Water fish, dry fish, cold fish, warm fish, all fish, dead fish.
Water dry cold warm all dead, all fish.
Fish food, fish money, fishy fish, fish all, fish none, fish, fish hiss like snakes,
like fish, all fish, different fish, all fish be, fish mead, fish mellow, fish sad,
fish angry, fish be all but gone. First fish, next fish, now fish all the same,
all fish different, like clownfish and another fish.
Now fish do not like fish but fish be fish so fish is fish, makes no sense
but fish be fish so makes sense like fish be fish how fish are not fish.
Brains are like fish, gray like fish, squishy like fish but not fish like how fish is fish.
Once upon a time there was a nonsensical fish.
It was a very small fish who lost easily and was friends with Eric.
The fish Eric was so tall like a skyscraper, talked like a fish but not a fish,
so odd it was a fish not being a fish but acting like a fish.
The tale of fish ending like a tale but started like nothing.
Like that would happen, more fish came and more fish left,
like a fish colony moving from ocean to beach.
Fish is odd but what isn't odd, if life is not odd but it is that's so interesting.
Makes no sense, that's a nonsensical poem from you.

A Perfect Princess
by Sara Pellegrino

Her hair
is the golden crown
from which the king placed on his head during ceremonies
Her eyes
are two calm beautiful seas
Her skin
the white snow
that cools your soul in the winter
Her face
is the magic sun
lights your thoughts and emotions
Her legs
are rampant horse
that travel the earth
Her dress
is the cattle the shepherd held
Her character, at times
a harsh mountain of frost,
But at other times,
a land filled with millions of flowers.

Bath Stairs
by Porter Leamons

An old man fell upon the stairs
And tumbled down with quite a scare
He landed hard and let out cries
Until he found a grand surprise
He fell into a bathtub deep
But not with water did he meet
Instead, he hit a bed of fries
And found himself in quite a guise
His pants were coated in grease
His hair was dotted with cheese
He looked around with great surprise
At this unexpected grand prize
He dug his hands into the tub
And tasted fries with such a rub
He smiled then let out a laugh
For hours he sat in there
Eating fries without a care
Until at last they had run dry
And he climbed out with a sigh
His clothes were stained with sauce and salt
But he knew it was his own fault
So off he went that jolly man
To tell his friends of what he'd planned

Writing
by Anabelle Pettinger

A flame in the darkness
A scroll of parchment
A quill, a typewriter
A pencil, a computer
Click, click, clack
Words appear
Messy ink
Ideas, thoughts, beliefs
Motivation, none,
Hope, inspiring
Love woven in,
Using the needle of words into the fabric of the World
Writing,
The flame thrown into a dark corner,
The air to a dying man,
The hope to a young girl,
It hurts us, it burns us,
But
We push back!
We Express!
We WRITE!

Mistaken Land
by Mary Moncibais

This house is for sale
It once grew haybales
The house had towering trees
The pollen made the farmer sneeze
Still the farmer loved that house
But he passed away as did his pork
Until his son came from New York
Then his son sold the home
And went back to his newest project
A football dome
The farmer still haunts the land
He does not be bland
His son did not want to carry on the tradition
So now the farmer is angry like ignition
And from the land of three thousand acres
Houses appeared an acre five neighbors
The farmer did not mind the mouses
But he hated and haunted the houses
Even today he wants his land back
But all he can do is make the floors crack
The houses never went away
It kept growing from that very day

Sun
by Breanna Crisan

A flame lit up the Earth
After a while, it died out, but
it always returns

Boo
by Cecily Payne

Oh, my cat Boo, how he smells like goo
he sleeps all day
He likes the name May
How grumpy is he
One day Boo scratched me
And he killed a bee
Why is he being bad, Boo is not rad
The next day he punched my knee
And he sat on me why is he being bad
Boo is not rad
On the last day of being mean
He scratched a tree and hissed at me
Why is he being bad
Boo is not rad
I tried to figure out why he was
Being mean then I saw a
Single flea it was controlling him
Now I will get rid of that single flea

Winter No More
by Dani Cohen

Winter, cold and dry.
The excitement of waking up to snow falling, falling, falling.
Layers of layers of clothes 'till you feel like a butterfly in its cocoon.
The feeling like you're in another world as you step out into the cold, icy snow.
The cold breeze whipping at your face.
Small white ice crystals in your hair, trying to catch them with your tongue,
Trees bare of leaves, coated in a thin layer of freshly fallen snow.
The delicious drink of hot cocoa right after a journey in the freezing cold.
This is winter, or at least what it used to be.
Fall and spring mixed together, but not winter.
Wet and humid days, there's no more snow,
No more winter jackets, no more sleigh rides, no more snow angels.
The temperature? Really high for winter,
Maybe it's not winter at all?
The effects of global warming are terrifying
It's taken away our winters, our forests, our water.
Something needs to be done before the effects worsen
Because there's no more winter at all.

New York City
by Mia Perez

The Big Apple
a tree, shining buildings,
and subway sightings

Christmas Eve
by Delaney Anderson

On window panes, the icy frost
leaves feathered patterns crissed and crossed,
but in our house the Christmas tree
is decorated festively
with tiny dots of colored light
that cozy up this winter night.
Christmas songs, familiar, slow,
play softly on the radio.
Pops and hisses from the fire
whistle with the bells and choir.
My dog is now fast asleep
on his back and dreaming deep.
When the fire makes him hot,
he turns to warm whatever's not.
Propped against him on the rug,
I give my dog a gentle hug.
Tomorrow's what I'm waiting for,
but I can wait a little more.

The Call of the Mountains
by Rachel Lang

There are places in the mountains
They call to me
I can see them, hear them, feel them
Like a soft breeze on my face
I feel a force swaying me to these gleaming places
Whenever I'm near them
The mountains hold such wondrous things
Crystal clear shining lakes
I could spend eternity sitting by the water
It's soothing, simply sitting and thinking
I row my boat far from shore
Into the great wide blue
As I glance up from the water
The mountains loom above
Rocky silhouettes that I can hear whispering my name
I yearn to go
Into the unknown, alone
Never looking back.

Willy
by Bristol Fulton

Willy oh willy, how your brown eyes glow
Willy oh willy, how your paint coat shows
You turn around that barrel as fast as you go
You run to the finish like there is no tomorrow
You make me so happy
So happy as can be
Please don't ever give me up
Please never stop loving me

The Many Emotions of Skydiving
by Julian Chouza

Nervous, Scared, Petrified,
Mama, I can't do this
Leg shaking, Palm sweaty, Fidgeting fingers
Julian, you got this
Skydiving, Windy, High up
Is it too late to turn back?
Suits, Timer, Enclosed glass area
Little kids laughing and having fun
Why am I so afraid?
My turn next
Don't know what to expect
Thrilled, Electrified, Excited
Mama! I did it!
Relieved, Reassured, No more fear
Julian! I knew you could do it!
Let's do it again

Rainy Day
by Noah John Lozuk

It's a rainy day. How much more boring can it get?
The wind blowing strongly not something you'll forget
When I peeked outside I saw tree branches falling,
It was like a sign Mother Nature was calling.
I finally stood up and got up from bed,
The school day was canceled it was something to not dread
I then opened the door and walked to the room,
And saw no one but a stick and a broom.
I then sat down at the kitchen table,
Where I saw one of my favorite fables.
The fable was from my dad
I then looked outside and it looked all sad
After all it was a rainy day,
Not the type to go out and play.
It was going to be very boring,
So I got up and started walking on the hardwood flooring.

What Nature Means To Me
by Lorianna Cipolla

Nice walks on the trail with my dogs
Amazing blue sky
Trees to pick apples from
Unimaginable fun in the pool
Racing bikes, riding horses
Eating outside with family and friends

Music Minds
by Sarah Bacon

It's like coffee
Addictive
Only stronger
Song lyrics carved into my brain like a stone
Albums and artists floating around
Songs always on repeat in my head
Always a song for everyone
References everywhere
She knows how it feels
That's why we're best friends
It can't get me anywhere
So for now it will sit there
Waiting to be used
Rotting
Crowding my mind
Maybe I should listen to the lesson
Hopefully I can remember my work next time

Movies
by Danyal Khan

Have you ever seen a movie?
Or been to the cinema?
Cus if you ever have,
You know what I mean.
The rush of the crowd
Hurrying to the movie.
The silence of the room
Like a sleeping mouse.
The brightness of the screen
When it's about to start.
The excitement of the people
When the best part comes on.
And as the movie ends,
The crowd's cheers and applause
Vibrate through your ear.
Now that the movie has ended
You walk away satisfied.

You
by Alexa Ralda

You,
Wonderful you.
Walking in the wind with you.
Talking with you,
for a seemingly endless time.
Playing frivolous games,
just for our amusement.
Oh how I wish we could spend more time with you.
But for now,
let me spend my time with wonderful you.

Heatherbirds
by Adriana Moreno

Elegant Sunflowers
sway,
As the wind whispers and sings.
It's the place I'd go,
Right where the Heatherbirds sing.
One would gaze at the stars,
One would swim in the sea,
One would lay in a field,
Right where the Heatherbirds sing.
For this place many would love,
Where the dear Heatherbirds sing.
In the fields of the free
it is where I would be,
For the stars all lead
To right where the Heatherbirds sing.

Penguin, My Cat
by Yuriko Rempel

At Night.
He sleeps.
Occasionally waking for the bathroom.
Sometimes sleeps in my room.
Sometimes wakes me in the middle of the night.
Sometimes he sleeps upstairs as he waits for my father to wake.
At Daytime.
He meows until his food arrives.
Biting, jumping, clawing until he can eat.
When I leave he sits in the sun and sleeps the day away.
As I come back from school he stands at the door meowing waiting for food.
I wait till six and then give him the food he craves.
Afterward, he sits high up in his cat tree
staring out the window at the birds that are not there.
Then he sleeps.

A Twisted Rainbow
by Shea Wirtenson

As I grow up,
And learn more and more,
I'm beginning to realize this world,
Isn't all rainbows anymore.
So many imperfections;
So much is wrong.
I realize now,
These aren't rainbows at all.
This what I'm living in,
It isn't rainbows; no.
What I'm living in now,
Is a twisted rainbow.

A Dream
by Emma Massa

I walk down the brown dirt road
Carrying with me a heavy load
Staring directly toward the sun
When all of a sudden the road is done
When I try to look forward all is blue
Just like the ocean and land doesn't loom
Then comes along a little boat
And when it stops it starts to float
It asks me which way I think it should go
and I simply reply I don't know
Then suddenly I wake up from my sleep
As my morning alarm starts to beep
So maybe it was all just a dream
Or was there more to it than it seemed.

The Deer
by Piper Hessong

As the river rushes past a lone deer
A cougar screams its cry of hunger.
The deer sprints home.
Not a worry in her mind
but still always aware of slight mistakes
she goes to her safe home
her sanctuary, where she rests
her speckled head, waiting for sunlight to come
she waits for the clover to bloom
and the grass grow lush
she lays her head down to rest
never to see the clover bloom
and the grass grow lush
all because she was alone, waiting for life to end.

How Can I Help
by Chloe Sanz

If you don't talk about what you're feeling, how can I help?
If you stay in your room holed up in your thoughts, how can I help?
If you put on your mask with your fake smile, how can I help?
If you stay lonely all alone, how can I help?
If you let your monster control you, how can I help?
If you can sleep with not a joyful mind, how can I help?
If you let your terrors make YOUR decisions, how can I help?
If you can't find a joyful thing in your broken sad heart, how can I help?
If you let your mind say terrible things about you, how can I help?
If you let your anxiety control you and your actions, how can I help?

Embrace
by Paul Foster IV

The end may be near, but you should embrace the ones you love.
You live forever, with someone, even if you aren't really there.
At least 2 people, that you don't even know,
love you, for who you are, and will remember you.
Don't be scared, be intrigued, to find what's next.
The life ahead, full of joy and less pain.
The pain here is nothing you should suffer from.
I wish I could've seen you. One. Last. Time.
We love you. We are with you. We are there.
Don't forget who I am, who you are, and who loves you.
You are with us, in our mind, and in our hearts.
Someone, maybe me, is always thinking of you.
The end may be near, but do not forget, we love you.
You live forever, with us.

Peace of the World
by Corinneanne Rogers

Peace that we give,
unconditionally to the world,
with love and affection,
can make world peace a perfection.
Peace spreads,
like a wildfire,
through people's hearts.
This world is a beautiful piece of art.
Love we give unconditionally form our hearts,
Even though sometimes our world is falling apart.
We just have to pick up the pieces and restart.
We can make a change if we adjust our view of the world.
The peace of the world is love,
but also affection, kindness, and politeness.
We must have trust in people and trust in ourselves,
To finally perfect world peace and make a connection.

What's In Your Socks
by Alysse Arnold

I have for you today a very special treat
It's one of my favorite things called stinky, smelly feet
The heel and ball, the top and bottom and of course the toes
Put off a pungent smell that can get stuck in your nose
Some are hairy, some are fat
Some are skinny, some are flat
Some are crooked, some are straight
Some have ten toes, some have eight
It is because of that I think they are so neat
One of my favorite things called stinky smelly feet

Alone With My Thoughts
by Aydin Phongluangtham

Ten minutes pass, and I don't know what to write.
Looking at the lantern, projecting light.
Twenty minutes pass, still sitting still.
Thinking about farmers, and the soil they till.
Thirty minutes pass, time comes to a halt.
Thinking about chefs with their pepper and salt.
Forty minutes pass, and I begin to ponder.
And I begin to wonder
Can boredom kill a human being?
What is the true cost of a diamond ring?
Fifty minutes pass, my hands under my head.
Alone with my thoughts, a time to question.
Alone with my thoughts, a time to think.
Alone with my thoughts, I go to bed.

Ocean Waves
by Ciara Hernandez

The waves come crashing on the shore
A sound of beauty that we adore
The water, blue as far as the eye can see
A scene so serene, it sets our souls free
The rhythm of the waves, a gentle hum
A lullaby that sings us to some
A dream land we can unwind
The waves, so beautiful, always on our mind
As we walk along the sandy beach
The waves roll in, with a graceful reach
It's hard not to stop and take it in
The beauty around, like a gentle embrace to win
So, let's bask in the sun, and let the waves roll
Feel the warmth and chill to our souls
The beach, so beautiful, it is hard to believe
That a world so serene, is ours to receive.

Hypocrisy Kills Morals
by Etta Crosman

Voices crying out to speak, like a bird inside a cage
Drowning in the pool of rejection and hypocrisy
Constrained by the view of society
Will we have a voice?
Will we be heard?
Losing lives to the lust of eyes
Hypocrisy kills morals,
Puts a chain around freedom,
But light shines through those cracks
Giving way to hope and joy

Gale Force Winds
by Lucian Saroyan

The autumn breeze.
Then smashing trees.
Blowing so hard,
The lumberjack flees.
The destructive gale
Makes all creations seem frail.
Dust swirls strong,
Putting leaves in throng.
But just as soon,
The sounds fade low,
Just to a blow.
All walk slow.
Through the autumn breeze,
and the smashing trees

Dribbling To the Finish Line
by Carl Tam

He dreams of playing in the NBA,
Dribbling and shooting day by day,
His heart is full of hope and drive,
And nothing can keep his dreams alive.
He practices hard and trains each night,
His heart and soul are in the fight,
He knows the path ahead is long,
And he believes he's strong.
He sees himself on the court one day,
Making plays that take our breath away,
His name is called, and the crowd roars loud,
He feels his feet touch the hardwood ground.
He rises high, above the rest,
His heart races, and he feels best
He shoots and scores, and the game is won
He's on top of the world, his journey's just begun.

My Grandma
by Alannah Sanchez

My grandma passed away 2 years ago today.
She was very sick at 100 years old,
I do miss her but I know it was her time to go.
I hope she is watching over me,
I hope she is protecting me from all evil.
I'm happy she's in a better place now!
No pain,
No suffering.
I love you grandma,
We will meet again soon

A Hot Summer Day
by Myra Look

The sun rays beam down
With the wind calm as a dove
I gaze around
And watch the trees dance
I sigh as I lay on my chair
Inhaling the scent of the summer breeze
I start to get thirsty
So I get up in a haste
I fly up the stairs
As I feel my hair flowing in the air
As I now absorb the summer breeze
I can't help but think
I can't miss this weather
Not even a blink

The Stars In the Sky
by Amelia Trejgis

The stars in the sky
Don't come from a firefly
They don't come from the streetlights
That shine in the lovely nights
These stars that you see
Are more beautiful than me
And wherever I go
They will always follow
When you look up at night
It's a beautiful sight
The stars in the sky are scattered
Which can make a pattern
Stars are very far away
But we still see them every day
Every night I go to bed
I say goodnight to my good old friend.

Ello the Smart Cat
by Erik Kristiansen

His fur is the color of the blazing sun
He prances around looking for fun
When he's outside his great adventure starts
And this is when he uses his smarts
He looks left and right when crossing the street
And feels the cold concrete below his feet
Then he hears a loud rolling noise
And leaps out the way all annoyed
He finds a pond full of astonishing fish
He catches one and puts it on a dish
He prances around with all of his glory
And this, is the end of the story

Food
by York Gladdess

I hold food with great love and affection
It brings me great delightful memories
Swimming in soup like I'm on vacation
It's been around for many centuries
Even when it's night, and the moon shines bright
Or in the daylight where the sun shines high
It's there, fill my tummy with delight
I like everything, and it's no lie
Yummy food from many different places
It feels like I'm there when I eat their food
It's nice to meet new people and faces
Food from your relatives just set the mood
Maybe you'll love it, or maybe you won't
Sit and enjoy your food with me, or don't

Fine
by Trulee Porter

You say you're fine but are you they ask if you are ok
but you put your head down and say i'm fine.
you just say it, it's not like they know what happened.
They think they know but they really don't
they assume you're fine but you're not.
You look down to say you're fine so when you look at them
in the eyes they don't see a tear. They ask you if you're fine.
You don't know what to say but you say yes so they don't ask any questions.
They walk away and leave you there you start to think why you said yes i'm fine.
Even when you really are not fine you stand up and start to walk away
from the tree that you sat by every day for the past month
thinking about everything that happened over the month
over the past few months you been sitting at that tree people came up to you
and asked questions but you put your head down so they walk away.

I Just Need To Be Me
by Justine Kendall

When did I become so ashamed?
Why do I feel this way? Why do I act this way?
I don't want to feel this way ...
I don't want to be the same as everyone, they say.
You have to feel the pain, you have to be great, NO!
I just need to be me; I just need to breathe and listen to the ones that love me.
All these lies have made me fall to the ground,
but I won't let them put me down.
I won't say goodbye to all my goals and roles in life.
I'll get back up, and I'll try and try again.
I'll wipe off the dried tears from my face and spread my wings
and fly to a world of happiness.

The Cycle
by Jaxson Brine

Oh summer, what a beautiful day.
Put your sweatshirt on, it's becoming fall.
The leaves will eventually decay.
The snow starts falling down like a big ball.
Everything is hibernating in holes.
Kids in the neighborhood, have fun sledding.
Please everyone, stay warm, go for your goals.
It's cold now, make sure you have good bedding.
The leaves are growing, the birds are blowing.
People on the street, calling and singing.
Oh my goodness, the water is flowing.
It's baseball season, the bats are swinging.
It's now summer, the cycle will repeat.
Our mission is officially complete.

I Wish, I Want
by Everett Sheldon

I want to be like the cool kids
They have the newest toys
I want to hang out with them
But I'm just an ordinary boy
I wish I could have millions of dollars, just to rub it in their face
I could buy a computer, a house, or even go to space
So I could brag to them about my stuff
So they would feel bad
I heard all they do is play video games
I bet their mom doesn't care
They spend all day
Just sitting in chairs
I wish I had their life
But at least I have a family who cares

Red Pandas
by Kyrin Toothaker

Creatures of red
They don't sleep in beds.
They love trees,
And they aren't free!
They don't shed,
Only their winter coat
Don't put them in boats
They can swim,
If I had a red panda I'd name it Kim!
Do red pandas have gym?

The Beautiful Colorado Mountains
by Stevie Caligaris

The beautiful Colorado mountains
Topped with glistening snow
The sky at sunset brings out the alluring colors of the mountains below
The beautiful Colorado mountains
So big and tall
The beautiful Colorado mountains
They're truly the best of all
The snow on the mountains like glitter
They're as peaceful as a hibernating bear
Oh, beautiful Colorado mountains
They are a beautiful sight
The beautiful Colorado mountains
Oh, what a delight

Music Brings People Together
by Chase Cates

Music is the thing that brings people together
Outside in the warm weather
It could be bad or boring but still it brings us together
The bird that flies around loses feathers
Because the music brings us together
The music must be right for it to be clever
Because some tunes can pull us far away from together
But the right lullaby can put us to sleep forever
Because music brings living things together
The spark of the world is music
And some people can lose it
But you must never forget
The best part of it Is the ly-rics
If you don't have good words
Then you might just get lured by the snake
So music brings people together
So listen to correct music forever

-Friends-
by Eunice Cristurean

Always connected, forever loyal.
Here to love us, and here to care for us.
Silly, weird, and understanding.
They're the ones who comfort us,
and the ones that we'll be with up above.
When we're sad, and when we're excited,
Always there to celebrate with us.
They're always here to lift us up.
We are ever grateful for them.

Free
by Jaxon Jensen

Everybody should feel free
Like a flying bumblebee.
We need to help find the key
And we can all accept each other finally.
There will be no more racism
There will be no more sexism
And nobody will be homophobic.
We should all feel happy
And never make anyone feel crappy.
Being nasty makes humans feel like
They have a horrible bite
We all must unite
So we can be free.

Wonderland
by Teddy Bacon

Beneath the waves, a world unknown,
A kingdom of the deep,
A wonderland.
Where sunlight fades and currents flow,
And creatures slumber into a sleep, calm and slow.
The coral blooms like gardens new,
In hues and colors of pink and blue,
The fish swim in a dance so serene,
Their movements like a dream.
A wonderland.
I am weightless in this place,
My breath a rhythmic sound,
Mesmerized in awe of beauty I embrace,
As I descend into a spiral,
bound ever down,
The sea, a whole new world.
A wonderland.
My soul feels alive, and grand.

Mother Nature
by Aliyah Ali

Mother of the Earth and its seven seas
She bore us with her strength and dignity
She is as beautiful as the landscapes she creates
And bestows the world with her ethereal beauty
Wherever she roams greenery flourishes alongside her
And her flowers deliver a perfumed aroma to our reach
She sends sweet songbirds who sing for us high up in the trees
And she provides delectable foodstuffs to nourish our desired needs
Forever nurturing us in this home eternally

I Am From
by Brianna Rizzo

I am from the land of the bald eagle
and native to the Big Apple.
I am from more than just places.
I am from experiences
from road trips across the country.
I am from being deep like the Grand Canyon.
I am from almost exploding like Old Faithful.
I am from exploring like Yellowstone.
I am from making my mark on the world like Mount Rushmore.
I am from not being afraid to hold my torch and
shed light of the truth like the Statue of Liberty.

Lilac In the Spring
by Pierre Saeed

Lily, lily in the fall
Greatest lily of them all
Lone as wheat but safe from crooks
This lily isn't as weak as it looks
Lily, lily in the winter
Cold as ice but none a splinter
When this lily is shivering cold
The roots underneath will dispose
Lily, lily in the summer
Great to none but not a bummer
Hot as fire but cool as springs
In the moonlight the lily sings
Lily, lily in the spring
Now the lily is thinner than string
Yet the lily refuses to lose
The lily lit its last fuse
Now the lily has become a lilac
Beautiful to all and a big tall stack
Yet the lilac hasn't changed
From inside it's still the same

My Childhood Toy
by Kimi Wang

When I was three years old,
I received a special instrument.
The orange color stood out to me so very bold,
The melody of the keys brought me joy.
Who would have thought that it was a toy?
The bright purple microphone echoing my voice,
When I saw it on the shelf, it was my first choice.
I hope one day to see it again,
I'd remember that moment every now and then.

Nature Is King
by Finn Hallissey

Nature sits upon a throne
Of branches and leaves
Only when the work is done does it roll down its sleeves
Nature sits there, sits and grieves
Upon its throne of leaves
Humans have stole its kingdom
Just like little thieves
Ax and saws with all their flaws
Humans kill birds and destroy their caws
The cause is to protect Nature

Snap Crackle Pop
by Brody Smith

I have all this doubt
and all i want is a way out
cause stepped on a lego
and I scarfed down an a ego
then I thought lego my ego
then I chopt do a tree but it would not come down
so I had a frown
on my face
So then I bought a new vace
then I smashed it with a mase
and then had to pay my mounthy fee
wanna be
A lax
Then I tripped on and axe
Then I bought a phone
A one that i now own
Then I busted the top
In snap crackle pop
I hope this song does not flop
On youtube
And I know kung foo

A New King
by Ethan Joseph

The king of the sky,
putting down its crown tonight,
For the moon to rise.

This Is Me
by Talulah LaMoure-Todd

Hair is auburn brown; it frizzes like a clowns
Eyes of emerald, green, blossoming like a tree
In spring. Limbs long and slim, and beautiful
Ivory skin. Smile like a breath of spring, voice
Soft like summer rain. Hands soft like flower
Petals, and a heart filled with kindness to the brim.
This is me; this is who I want to be!

Profound Words
by Lily Mendez

Life is like a tree
A tree that sways in the breeze, wavering at even the slightest touch of insolence
Delicate branches reaching out for the feel of love and motivation of courage
Sometimes, leaves fall and die, but they grow back
Roots stretch and recoil
Such as whispers of life scan the horizon for even the faintest trace of reassurance
Seeds drop
And new growth appears
After a millennia, the journey ends
With a sickening crack and the crunch of a fallen giant
Supplying the bare needs of its executors

Cars
by Creed Brown

Cars, cars running everywhere
Drinking up lots of gas
Cars, cars running everywhere
Their radios playing bass
Cars, cars running everywhere
In all different shapes and sizes
Cars, cars running everywhere
Taking people to all different places
Cars, cars running everywhere
Running all over the nation
Cars, cars running everywhere
A vital transportation
Cars, cars running everywhere
Drinking up lots of gas

Flow
by Brahm Wheeler

The little river
flowing through the soft, moist ground,
Granting life to us

Sometimes
by Lily Davis

Sometimes I look in the mirror and all I can see is scars.
Sometimes I think I need the scars for attention.
Sometimes I think I need the scars to keep sane.
Sometimes I realize I may be a bad person.
Sometimes I wonder if I deserve them.
Sometimes I wish I could see past the scars.
Sometimes I don't want to focus on things that only happen sometimes.

Twins
by Alyson Tallman

Sally, Sally, greenish hair
Sally, Sally, do you dare
Sally, Sally, fell down the stairs
Barbra Ann, Barbra Ann, running for mayor,
But she can't because she found Sally passed out at the bottom of the stairs.
Sally, Sally, dreaming of bears
Barbra Ann, Barbra Ann, dreaming to be mayor
Sally, Sally, dead as can be
Barbra Ann, Barbra Ann, crying to me
Sally, Sally, up and ready
Sorry Sally, forgot you were deady

Foundation
by Hadley Taylor

Everyone needs a foundation
Everyone has their own
We use it as our legislation
It makes us feel known
Some are friends
Some are educational achievements
It purely depends
I imagine there are no disagreements
Sometimes its music
Sometimes they can blend
No one gets to pick
Our foundation decides what we intend
Our whole reputation
Is all in our foundation

Flowers
by Avery Glaser

The center of a sunflower smells like fresh honey off a hive.
The petals look as if someone has hand painted them.
Dandelion petals flow in the wind as the costumes flow on dancers.
They smell like the end of winter and the start of spring and shorts.
A rose cycle is as elegant as the cycle of life.
When you stroke the petals it sounds like a slight breeze in the summer.
Poppys are as bright as the sun on a nice summer day.
Flowers are the peace the earth needs.

Mother
by Rosselin Saravia

Watch as she comes home
like a beaten up dog
her eyes all drowsy but gives it her all to be happy
feel all her passionate kisses and her warm heartfelt hugs
she treats you like a princess but you take it for granted at times
she tries to make the best of it
even from the littlest of things
when she hears you weep
and howl like a wolf
she feels your pain even more than you do
she gave you the beautiful gift of life
and cares for you like a bear and her cub.

Fear of the Unknown
by Josue Reyes

In this world, there are many things to fear.
Like snakes or spiders, everyone you know may disappear.
You could lose a loved one.
Flee from your home and have nowhere to run.
Having the fear of losing a valued possession,
or do something wrong and give a bad impression.
To feel timid in the highest of places.
You could be lost on this planet without any traces.
You might be afraid of death alone,
and just be afraid of all the unknown.
Be afraid of work and all of school.
Get embarrassed in front of people and be called a fool.
It could be something simple, not anything too big.
Like a roach or cow, or maybe even a pig.
Whatever it is that you may fear,
it may affect you but don't make them severe.
I've told you about the things many people may fret.
They're something that takes time for you to forget.
Don't let them stop you from achieving your dreams.
Fears are really not all of what they seem.

Deep In the Amazon
by Bryar Land

A bobcat stirred in the underbrush as an eagle circled scanning for mice.
A lost weary traveler scarred from battle sauntered through the jungle
unaware of the dangers that lay ahead.
A tiger twitched its tail startling our young friend, causing him to step back
and trip on a root, falling onto a mossy bed of sticks,
disturbing a hill of bullet ants. Screaming, he scrambled in desperation
pulling himself up as a huge ball python slowly wrapped itself around him.
As he gulped his last breaths, he fell down into a grave
of ferns, underneath a kapok tree.

Nature
by Teodora Milinovic

What would the world be without
the over complicated meanings that now define us?
Would we be like lions in the field, killing for the survival of our family?
Would that life, without our new meanings, be more rich?
Would it be more fulfilling to live by the very laws of nature?
Only those with the experience of both worlds can tell,
while the rest of us listen and think,
and ask ourselves questions in every context,
seeking all of the answers the world has to offer,
from a lion, a deer, and a family of beavers.
Maybe even our own minds.
This is why we have the priceless power of growth,
acquiring knowledge and learning. Or maybe it's just our own intuition?

Leavin' Seasons
by Aubrie Bacio

The air sat thick around the windowsill
The boredom seemed to be God's will
The leaves detached from the trees
Giving in to the rough breeze
The Autumn was lively, but not for long
The Winter now begin before it is continued
Snowflakes danced in the air, on the floor
Not to be seen, neither nor
They melt slowly when they meet warmth
All around the cold wharf
The Spring sprouts much needed flowers
Lifting smells in the air in beautiful showers
Sun shining bright
Letting yellow light spurt lovely rays of bright light
Spring is beautiful, but a great climax is setting in
So now Summer may begin
The season of sunshine and smiles
Shines bright for miles

Lightning Bug
by Lexi DelCurto

As the bug lights up so bright
I begin to wonder how it's butt acts like a light

Volleyball
by Shamaya Ferch

Playing as a powerful team
Having an amazing attitude
Terrific teammates
Terrible teammates
Keeping my head up high
Encouraging each other
Hitting hard
Serving strong
Spiking sharply
Cheering cheerfully
Pass the ball between the players
Three in front
Three in back
Six smiling players
Set to spike
Spike to score
The final score we fight to win
I love volleyball

My World
by Elisha Hupfer

You know what gets me up in the morning?
Not the birds, the grass, or the trees
But the hope I have in this country
And what it will do for me.
See this place we call home
It's the only one we've got
So we have to care and protect it
No matter what.
But right now we are broken
And need to come together
Because in the end
We need to fight for each other.
See divided we fall
We can't make a stand
But united we WILL rise
And stand together hand in hand.
See I want to make a difference in this world
Maybe you want to change it too
So I'm gonna ask you this question,
What do YOU want to do?

Winter Wonderland
by Gillian Levy

As snow falls
On majestic trees
Quiet is the sound

Here At Last
by Leila Tarleton

Mountains-
Tall and Vast,
made to last
Foxes, Owls, through the night
leaving small critters
with a fright
Snowmelt Creeks
Rushing past
Wildflowers
Blooming fast
Glad that Summer
is here
AT LAST!

The Static T.V.
by Colin Crichton

Sitting on my armchair
Waiting for the show to turn on
Many years I waited
Waited for the show to turn on
Waiting for the hope
Waiting for the peace
Waiting for the static to stop
Wondering what horrors it has to tell
Woe, are my days
Sitting on my armchair
The show I don't know
Where life is of the essence
When the tides of time crash on you
The static stops
A bird appears to me
Flying, over my T.V.
Not a small bird, not a large bird
Not a scary bird, not a plain bird
Nothing strange
I ask of it, "Please, fix my T.V!"
Until it lies, dead on the T.V.
How could this happen to me!
Sitting on my armchair
Wait a static T.V.

If You Can
by Elijah Sendi

If you can be good at something and do it every day.
Then you shall break away from it bit by bit and then continue it.
If you can be the person who you are, you're the very one
to not listen and break who you are for a bit.
If you can tell a lie with a straight face
you can't be trusted without a doubt
until opening the gates and accepting your fate.

From Summer To Winter
by Ethan Cecil

I love the grassy plain
With the grass swaying to and fro
But what have I to gain
When it is all covered with snow?
I love the ocean wide
With the waves tumbling down below
But I'll have time to bide
When the ice begins to grow.
I love the forest deep
With the birds that sing and roam
But when winter brings sleep
I will have to go home.

Inside
by Syrenna Keeling

Soaring above the earth
The stars so bright above
Upon a feathered wing
Engulfed with the wrath of fire
Inside it is
With battle, death and tears
With music and dancing
So fierce and strong
Yet so merciful and calm
Inside it is
The gentle flow of water
The elegance of the cool breeze
Turns to a tsunami, in an instant
Inside it is
So many things hurling around
Yet so calm and peaceful
This is the place I escape to, this is my world
It is a wonderful place and it is mine
For this place I speak of
Is my mind

Life
by Lucy Frost

Isolation
Lonely, Unwanted
Hurting, Betraying, Distracting
Never ever leaving your side
Creating, Talking, Bonding
Nurturing, Connected
Company

Soccer
by Rowdy Ryser

The ball whips through the air
The side of your foot
Hits the ball, runs through the air
To hit the back of the net
Running to the corner
Celebrating with your friends
The crowd is going crazy
Dribbling to the next
You kick it up and over
The goalkeeper and slides on the
Back of the net to win
The score is two to zero

The Perfect Melody
by Alaska Shaw

When I turn on my favorite tunes,
I hear the most beautiful sounds
Weaving a golden tapestry.
The voice, expressing its deepest desires
In a never-ending riddle.
The guitar, with every strum
Adding crisp clear drama.
The piano, persisting in the background
Clarifying a catchy tune.
The drums, like a heart
Beating out their passion.
The violin, while being stroked
Giving smooth, direct emotion.
The flute, gently whistling,
Mimicking nature's sounds
When all these come into harmony
Adding some, taking some away
Until a balance is reached
A perfect melody-
Until reality calls me back.

Soulless Animals
by Fo Venne

Soulless zombies
Staring at their phones
While someone is yelling for help
Absorbed in their own tiny worlds
That fit into a pocket
The pockets of cargo pants made for the workers that build our city every day
Brick by Brick
The pockets of cargo pants that were made to be worn
once by the citizens of the internet

Shadows
by Ava Paiz

The shadows began to dance and flicker across the building
with the fading and setting sun
They expand in wisps and tendrils, beckoning, almost begging to be acknowledged.
No remorse, no regret for the things it devours
The alleyways crawl with such shadows, such vile creatures
The night is their domain in the city, with no light to combat it
They reek of disease and decay, a suffocating silence
There is no light at the end of the tunnel
For the phantoms of the dark show no mercy to the angels of light

The Pain I Feel
by Izabell Whitney

The pain I feel is unbearable.
I deal with my problems, divorce, fighting, fake people, getting bullied, called ugly.
I never see my dad because he made mistakes that made it so I can't see him a lot.
My dog died right after the divorce then we got a puppy
and it got attacked and died.
And it got to the point I hated myself.
I still do for all the mistakes I have made and I have to act like
I'm good all while really breaking down and want to let it all out but if I do then ...
"I suck, I just want attention, I'm a pick me and I have been told
to go kill myself, hang myself, that I'm worthless,
that I don't belong in this world."
I don't know how people don't see what's wrong with me,
but I trust no one because now I'm at the point of not being able
to talk to anyone about anything because it gets around
and I just say I'm fine and get on with my day.
I don't talk to the counselor because I don't trust them no matter what.
One time I hid in my room and ... I don't want to talk about it
and people act like my mom and stepdad don't know, but they do.
They also think it's funny to talk about it.
But I'll get on with my life like an everyday thing.

The Sad Truth of Modern Day Dinos
by Trenton Wickham

Back then.
They could rule as far as their eyes could see
from the blue sky to the deep depths of the sea.
But now,
They're farmed and butchered for their eggs and meat,
How did these great beasts meet their defeat?

From Time To Time
by Elijah Cox

From time to time we dream of stars.
From time to time we get scars.
From time to time we have peace.
From time to time we suffer from defeat.
From time to time our days are filled with luck.
From time to time our days really suck.
From time to time we have the sun shine bright.
From time to time we have thundering nights.
From time to time we are happy, sad, angry, and glad.
From time to time we show love and hate.
But from time to time I think we need to learn how to
appreciate the pros in life so let's focus on the good times.

Why Did You Have To Go
by Summer Dostie

I loved you so much Grandpa.
I really miss you.
I wish I could see you.
I had a lot of fun when you were around.
I wish you could see me, my sister and our brother.
our brothers are turning 3 years old, my sister is turning 10, and I am turning 12.
I know you are still here watching all of us in heaven
I can't wait to see you when I'm in heaven, every time I go to your house I tear up.
I know you can hear me, I know that you love me and I know that you all of us.
I love you and when I have hard days I can talk to you no matter what
cause you're always there for me and my family.
I'm so glad that you were in my life.
I can't believe you had to go I loved you so so so so much.
I know you love me and I love you
and I know you love me, my sibling, and my mom and dad.
I wish you where at the wedding so you could see me and my family.
I really wish I was up in heaven with you and Grammie.
I know Grammie is also watching me and my family.
I love you, we all do.
I love you my angel.

School
by Saadya Blumenthal

Off to sea,
a farewell,
a goodbye for me.
Cold waves splash across my face,
thunder crashing,
palms sweating on the helm.
Darkness fills the sky,
darker than the pupil of an eye.
My heart beating,
like the time I have.
Tears pour, racing across my face.
When will it end?
Finally,
the bell rings.
I run faster than the speed of light.
The freedom in my heart
carries strength so great.
I am finally free.
Warm.
And home at last.

The Babbling Brook
by Sydney Smith

There was a babbling brook
Where I would sit under the trees
My journal in hand
Letting the stanzas
Flow through my fingers.
And then the world spun
No longer was it rich and green
But gloomy and gray.
There was no babbling brook
But in its place
A dried up river bed
With trash overflowing.
I travel the world
And instead of writing about the beautiful Earth
I write about the trash
That piles around me
And instead of my words
Jumping around on my page
They sink in and lie there
Waiting for death to take them away.

Playoffs
by Sterling Sherburne

The stadium rumbles
With the cheer of fans
And people are jumbled,
all in the stands
They make their way
Across to their seats
Ready to stay,
and watch players compete
Teams dash onto the field
Waving up to the crowd
Ready to wield
Their metaphoric crown
They want to win this game,
no matter what
For it would be a shame
If they didn't make the cut
To be the best in the league
Would be amazing indeed
They will finish fatigued,
But will have won indeed

Me
by Hannah Lyslo

My name is Hannah,
And I don't like bananas!
Sports are my life,
So this is what I write.
Basketball, dribble, shoot, and score:
After this poem, you will be wanting more!
Family of four and a cat named Rudy.
Don't mess with me because I can be moody.
I have brown hair,
And my eyes are pretty rare.
Brown, green, and blue in my eyes,
I'm pretty honest but tell some lies.
I love the color red,
And I love mornings in my bed!
Track, soccer, swimming and more,
Besides all that, my life's a bore.
Going to school and learning about God,
He forgives my sins even towards my mom!
Playing clarinet for four years
This is the end, turn off your listening ears!

An Open Book
by Madelyn Landes

Browsing the shelves
to take a look
What book?
Kings or peasants?
Desolate or carefree?
Reality or fantasy?
Ancient or modern?
I pick a tale and begin to devour the words.
Like a skillfully woven tapestry
the storyline unfolds
I am drawn into the magic of an open book.
Hours pass. I am unaware.
a tale like magic
dong, dong, dong
Wait! is it really that late?
rushing, out of the library
back home.
regretful to leave the novel
tomorrow, back to the wonderful world
of an open book.

The Night I Was Alone
by Vincente Ramirez

It was one dark night
Although she was bright
We would always fight
Never could stop staring in those eyes
I can still hear her cries
Never will I stop liking you
I feel blue and I want to sue
You for breaking my heart
I will be smart, this time
I can only hear the chime of the clock
the sound of time as it ticks and it tocks
I think of her mismatched socks
Reminds me of good moments
It should've been a crime for loving you
the time I was hugging you
The time I got the flu
You were always there for me
Now I'm free to be
With Whom I choose
I'm singing the blues, tonight.

Oh, What a World
by Jennalee Garcia

Oh what a world,
In which I must observe.
I watch them;
Longing for what I cannot have,
While I continue to reserve.
I look up at the sky wondering,
Simply wondering,
"Why?"
"Why was I cursed with such despair?"
"Couldn't I be happy
with a life that is fair?"
Although my surroundings were glorious,
I still bleed internally.
Watching them as they pass
only reminds me of what I worry.
So now I sit,
Alone again.
Realizing that one day,
My fears will pass;
And I will be at bay.

Finding Your True Self
by Ahna Ventimiglia

When I'm lost
I'm stuck
My feet are planted
My mind is somewhere else
and all there is, is a voice of negativity
I'm lost with negative thoughts
I am trapped in my own brain
My anxiety takes control
And I am useless
But then another voice pops in my head
I am one
I am me
And I am awesome
And no one can tell me what to do
I found myself
I found my mind
I found my voice and that voice
Will make me feel free
When I am found, I am no one else
Than me

A Beautiful Sight
by Emily Peters

It is dark
I hear dogs bark
The light that shined bright
Shutoff and became night
The colors in the sky
Make something new
The clouds in the sky
make a beautiful view

Late Night Drive
by Tyler Hohlman

When the weather's cold.
Time does stop.
Everything is sold.
And there is no clock.
It's just you and me.
While we wait,
With a song called "we"
Without hate.
Us in the car
The world may wait,
Because we will go far.
For us it is straight.

The Digital Depression
by Quinn Schlesinger

In a dark room
At the top of the stairs
Late at night
Misery is spreading under the cover of fake experiences and plastered on smiles
A girl wades through the river of poison
Instead seeing it as a field of daisies
She thinks it's a way
To learn about others
But instead it is really
A messed up mirror shoving her in
The wrong direction
She's trapped under the ice
Falling into the darkness
On the glowing screen
She is scrolling, scrolling, scrolling
She is pulled in by the digital depression
Of social media

The Missing Ice Cream
by Madeline Johnson

I have eaten
All the ice cream
That was in
The freezer
And which
you probably were
Saving
For dessert
Forgive me
they were delicious
so soft
and so sweet

Sleep
by Everly Specht

Sleep is a thing
that takes you away
to a place where you
can dream until the
world startles you
back
your fluffy pillow
massages your head
until your eyes float
back down, and your
dreams come back to you

Thinking of Spring
by Harper Baxter

A man in his thoughts
Flowers and butterflies in his dreams
But while it's winter,
Thinking about spring,
A man can only dream
All the colors in his thoughts,
Show in his character,
When he walks into the room,
Everyone brightens up
If you ever pass this man,
You are in luck
For this man will help you see
The darkness in winter also has the
brightness of spring.

Dancing Food
by Chloe Gebhard

Bread and Butter danced,
and pranced as they sang together.

High Tides and Good Vibes
by Josephine Chiaramonte

Inspiring sunset
An intelligent calm dolphin leaps
Over the water

Llama
by Alexia Amaro

Llama
So soft and cute
So fast, kind, and stinky
I feel like I am warm and safe
Nature

School
by Haevyn Pelton

School's like a pound
We live with the hounds
Teachers say "pay attention
Or you'll end up in detention"
Oh we make a sound

A Place Like Home
by Ava Welch

A place that doesn't need a bed or your own space to feel like home
A place that is old and not up-to-date
but still have the comfort of your bed after a hard day
A place with more memories than people could imagine
A place where you can go on the worst days or the best day and still feel at peace
A place where I look up to the people around me
A place where firsts were taken, first swim to catching your first fish
A place where freshly made beds put you to sleep like a baby in a swaddle
A place where Gramp's magic hammer or duct tape could fix anything
A place where Grammie's cookies could make any day better
A place you don't need to call home to have it feel like home
A place called camp

Colorado Nature
by Carson Broccardo

The mountains so purple with majesty,
The peaks so white with snow,
The trees covered so lusty,
The birds in a row.

Shark
by Daniel Bozora-Meadows

Swimming in the ocean
Hammerhead shark
Apex predator
Rapacious (aggressively greedy or grasping.)
Killing machine

Losing
by Zavier Miller

Losing
Is such a drag.
While the winner,
They start to brag.
This can make one
Upset or worse.
But don't worry,
There is a source.
To winning that is.
To get better too.
Just practice, practice, practice.
That's all there is to do.

Dance
by Whitney Steibel

We both met dancing on the sidelines, not being as good as the others
We continue to dance even when it was hard or frustrating
The music flowed inside of us making the steps so much easier
We danced along with the rhythm, not caring about anything else in the world
The world fell away and it seemed like it was just us
dancing to the music with no care in the world
The music began to consume you, like the water in a pool
Even though we were on the sidelines, to us,
we were on the front and center of the stage, just us dancing with the music

3rd
Place

Erika Powell

The Unmistakable Mirror
by Erika Powell

Look at yourself in the mirror,
but not too long.
15 seconds is all it takes for insecurity to spark,
then spread like a wildfire, impossible to put out.
Wild red flames of unease,
steamy glows of depression,
scorching torches of worries flaring up the sky,
smoke intoxicating clouds of inspiration,
turning the bright sun of happiness dark.
The towering burning trees begin to shrink
and shrivel until they're nothing.
Just like you.
The mirror stares at you too long.
You hate it and the glass hates you,
but time and time again you go to it.
Each time it makes you shrink even more into the misery of your body.
It breaks your fragile, fragile confidence that takes so long to build up.
Go back into society and pretend.
That's all you can do after you face
the unmistakable misery of a mirror.

Wellspring Thomas

The Land of the Forgotten
by Wellspring Thomas

In the Land of the Forgotten
Rivers of buttons and beans
Childhood toys in between the cushions of the couch
Cloudy skies of painted rainbows and stars
Stuffed animals of sleepy safety
Doors to attics you never explored
Nighttime stories underneath the comfort of a blanket-fort
Hikes into the woods with your older brother
Rock collections and Honeysuckle flowers
Unfinished sketchbooks and fairy tales of maidens in towers
You look back at all of these things
with a combination of nostalgia and disarray
But beware if you venture too far
You may forget about Present Land
A land of fear and joy
Sadness and anger
Stress and relief
And most importantly
You

Rylee McKinney

Rylee wins $100 for her first-place finish
in the grade 7-8 division with her poem, "All I Know Is Blue."
An emotional piece,
exploring the consequences of allowing others
to dictate the way we feel about ourselves.
Great work, Rylee!

All I Know Is Blue
by Rylee McKinney

I never looked good in blue
until you took all my colors away
you stole the red that once painted my cheeks
when I would laugh a little too hard
the gold in my hair that you never liked
is now a faded dull brown
even the green that once shone in my eyes
appears a melancholic blue
before you I avoided blue
because I knew
it didn't complement my vibrancy
now blue has consumed me
all I know is
blue

Division III

Grades
8-9

Sunsets
by Hemani Singh

Beautiful sunsets
Creating ombre effects
Beauty in the colors.
Touching the hot sand
As the wind flows through my hair
Beauty at the beach.

A Shelter From the Troubles of Life
by Leona Arnold

Home
Never felt so perfect
(love floating through every space)
Never felt so loving
(Our living room, gray and perfect as it is
The grand t.v. and the couch so comfy
The movie nights spent with family
Popcorn we find hidden in the couch
The days spent playing video games)
Never seemed so out of harm's way
(In our cozy neighborhood)
My bedroom overruled by chaos
Cluttered with books of all kinds
The stuffed animals that keep me safe
A memory wall laid out with pictures
The assortment of blankets to keep me warm
My hideout
Our front lawn
Ever so green, filled with memories
A place to escape
The backyard strung with lights
Our own getaway
My father's Mississippi Roast
A heavenly food
My momma's German Dumplings
Once in a blue moon do we get them
And the laughter
A sound of love
With every joke or sign of happiness
The thrill of a game
Or an awkward moment broke by laughing
This tension relieved by joy
A room filled with warmth
After a day that was tough
Telling us that we are safe
This home is a refuge or
A shelter from the troubles of life

Time O'clock
by Olivia Castaneda

Oh time, how it eats you up
Or breaks you down
I need time to breathe
To realize what is happening in front of me
By the time I realize
Time is already gone
Down the drain
Oh, how time flies by like a Hummingbird's wings
In the fresh spring breeze
This is how I feel
When I am with you
The only time when I slow down
Is when I feel like I am going to drown
Oh, how slow time goes when wanting
To flee or, for once have time fly.
The minutes seem like hours
The hours feel like days
This is how I feel
When I am away from you

Outrage
by Lejla Omeragic

i am so mad
this world has been through so much
why did we become so bad?
why is that we can't save the good?
we just stood.
our humble home is falling
i'm not sure, seems like death is calling.
i say "we" because there is not only one
who could've done what has been done
there isn't one gun
that doesn't have the right to hurt a ton
i'm sorry to that daughter or son
whose life has barely even begun,
and are already told to run ...
why are we told to not make a sound?
we better stand our ground.
i will not let my future fall
for i hope my children get their chance to stand tall.
But without change, I will keep feeling this outrage
how strange, can't we flip the page?
find a way to outweigh these ways?
we must unite as one
to reveal a brighter, bolder more beautiful day,
or we will keep dying this way.

So What
by Maddie Gonzales

What have we come to -
A world overflowing with spite and anger?
A world that feels the continuous need to resort to violence?
A world impotent to accept others for who they truly are?
A world so detrimentally separated
It may never be able to mend itself back together?
What have we come to -
A world revolving around a glowing box
Sitting tirelessly in front of strained eyes?
A world brimmed with shamefully unrealistic standards?
A world in constant fear of the horrors viewed on the news?
What have we come to -
A world crippling under the constant oppression of human destruction?
A world subjugated with superfluous waste?
A world so focused on the present
It is unable to see its pernicious effect on the future?
So what,
I ask you,
What have we come to?

Hi Spring!
by Valerie Becerril

Spring arrives on tiptoe,
Softly creeping through the land,
Whispering secrets to the earth,
With gentle touch and loving hand.
The air is alive with fragrance,
As flowers bloom in brilliant hues,
And birdsong fills the morning,
With melodies both old and new.
The trees awaken from their slumber,
Stretching out their leafy arms,
Reaching for the warming sun,
Embracing all of nature's charms.
As the days grow longer,
And the warmth of springtime spreads,
We shed our winter layers,
And turn our faces to the sky instead.
The earth is reborn with color,
The rivers flow with life anew,
And we are reminded of the beauty,
That nature brings into our view.
So let us revel in this season,
This time of hope and growth,
And let the wonders of springtime,
Fill our hearts and souls with both.

Depression
by Nevaeh Pease

Depression is something we have no control over
It's not all in our heads like some people say
It's something that takes control over our lives
It can be caused by anything in life and then when people say
we don't want to do anything because we are just lazy,
that's not true because we do, just we are so down and sad
that we just want to crawl up in my bed and cry
I can't, my body won't let me and the meds don't help
That don't make me happy nor sad in life so I draw blood
to feel something in life, but all I feel is numb in life
So why do I have this life? And my friends think I'm going to kill myself
so I won't feel the pain in life like the tears in my eyes
Drawing blood from my wrists.
Life, the world, depression the world
Is just a black blur and that's just the world

The Mask
by Penelope Gonsalves

Spring
The season of what they call our mask of "Joy"
Only the mask sees
The Sunshine finally peaking through the shadows
Only for the mask to see
The new bright flowers flooding the land
Only for the mask to smell
The air fresh as the bright blue ocean
Only for the mask to hear
Birds chirping happy songs
Only for the mask to hear
"Spring is perfect"
Only the mask says
Adrenaline only hits the denser parts of the mask
till it breaks
Yet it still
cannot get to me
I cannot see sunshine
Only the shadow
I cannot smell the new bright flowers
Only the sad sours ones left behind
I cannot breath the fresh air in my lungs
Only the frigid air that burns my chest
I cannot hear the birds chirping happy songs
Only the sad birds left behind to chirp sad songs
"Spring is scary"
Only I ever say
When the masks breaks

Left Out in the Rain
by Maddie McLagan

Rain washed away the care of everyone else
Rain pouring, they're running away
And I'm left out there.
Though even after the rain you're still there
Not washed away like all the others,
Still okay with my broken, cracked heart,
Not minding my broken, shattered brain
Comfort like I never felt before.
Then finding others who don't mind the storms
Who like sticking by me even in the thunder
Lightning streaking int he sky
I thought they're going to leave but all are still there,
all of them bracing the storm with me
and are still standing out there in the rain with me
Eyes of comfort like the pine woods and stormy seas
Hugs of warmth like a summer's breeze.
Making sure we're all ok before ourselves,
Even if we were hit by the lightning first
Thank you for bracing the storm with me, My friends.

I Was Born Who I Am
by Sophie Zhou

Hair as black as the night's air
Eyes slanted, long and dark
A nose that's flat not fair
I stand out like a glimmering, yellow spark
Proud of my appearance, unique, exquisite, rare
A reflection of my background and roots
But always am I met with stares and glares
As if my looks are something to dispute
Pressure is a shadow looming over a mountain high
To be the best at everything, no matter the pain
And every time I try to reach the sky
I fall and fail in society's absolute disdain
The need to fit in with the white, to ignore views of those
who can't see past my birth
To reach unbelievable academic height,
but balance a culture so rich and diverse on this earth
Yet we blaze a trail, where we've yet to go for we are the essence of the dragon fire
With roots that run deep, and hearts that glow that fuels
the soul and ignites our desire
Rising from the East with grace and might
We stand tall and face the world with pride
In a culture steeped in tradition and light
For we are Asian, graceful, wise and true
with open hearts and spirits that won't hide

Be Kind
by Bryson Martin

A long time ago,
Back in the old day,
People were nice
In a friendly neighbor way.
But now something is different
Something has changed.
The manners of people
Have become deranged.
People must be nice
Just like they were before,
Or the world will again crumble
And be thrown into war.
Say please and thank you,
Mind your p's and q's.
And when you use your manners,
They'll spread like the fly
To everyone all around you.

Not a Big Deal
by Athena Jimenez

Supposedly we are kids on a mission
For a great education
In addition to the condition we work our backs off
I'm sorry, I think you're holding us back
This can't last
That's not supposed to make us laugh
But I'm sorry, you don't understand
We'll never stand, get up, what a weird hill to die on
You're wrong, it's not a big deal
But it'll always be a big deal,
It's never about how we feel
I hope you never yell again, Then overhear jokes
I know you know it's all a joke At least I hope
But oh! Hey! Where did my right to opinions go?
Way in that closet nobody goes in,
And we'll never win when kids like us are nowhere close
Those dreams went to the ground when they found
How messed up your classes are
How hard you make this
Listen to this craziness, Laziness is not out excuse
We're not used to it, Here it's different
Living in a nightmare, A never ending hall
Never standing so tall, we'll scream, no sound comes out, Nothing out loud
But with how loud you yelled I'm scared
Why should I care? Call out criticism like it's hate
We wait for the day things will hopefully change. Will they

The Spring Breeze
by Ngozi Uche-Konkwo

The spring breeze blew, soft and light,
Through fields of green, so fresh and bright.
But in her heart, a storm raged on,
A pain that never seemed to be gone.
The girl walked on, with heavy feet,
Her heart weighed down, her soul replete.
The world around her was in bloom,
But she felt trapped in her own gloom.
The birds sang sweetly, high above,
But her heart felt broken, devoid of love.
The sun shone down, warm and bright,
But her world was shrouded in endless night.
The wind whispered, a soft caress,
But for the girl, it was all a cruel test.
A reminder of a love gone by,
A hope that seemed too far to fly.
But still she walked on, with heavy feet,
Her heart weighed down, her soul replete.
The world around her was in bloom,
But she felt trapped in her own gloom.

Craving
by Madisen Madsen

I was kneeling on the ground, feeling empty and cold, I felt at if I was in
the room by myself but thousands surrounded me.
I could feel my faith fading.
My hands went numb as the both of you grabbing them so gently,
my vision was blurry,
I looked up and saw two smiles I longed to see for years.
Your wings wrapped around me, to shield me from everyone, I was only focused
on the ones I saw in front of me. The ones that gave me the smile
I once had on my face, you looked whole, untouched by the world.
I wasn't scared as I saw you kneeling with me, it felt as if you were there.
I couldn't breathe, I started crying even more than before but I knew I wasn't sad.
I knew he was happy again with you by his side.
There was a piece missing in his heart
That you finally got to fill. I closed my eyes when I opened them again
The presence of the both of you was gone.
Her smile was more beautiful than I imagined
The smile I saw on your face was so real, so wholesome, and sweet.
I didn't want them to go, I wasn't ready to let go again
I wasn't ready to see your face fade away, I didn't want to say goodbye.
My faith was back but you were gone ... once again.
How does a child live without their parents? If only you could speak to me
The smiles were magical but oh how I wanted your words, I craved advice.
One more time ... I wish for just one more time.

The Wolf of Three
by Ivy Wess

The moon is a bright white bowl in the midnight sky
and the wolves would howl with fur of white,
right near the willow caught by the breeze
near the shining waters just like the sea,
up in the mountains right past the trees,
there stands a wolf that represents three,
one for the moon in the midnight sky,
one for the willow that breezes by,
one for the waters just like the sea
all of those things represent three,
her fur is like the moon soft gentle white,
her howl catches the breeze all through the night,
her eyes glisten like the water from the sea,
her kindness shines bright like the galaxy,
if you follow the moon to willow tree
swaying its branches and beautiful as can be.
Near the tree, you will see the waters,
the shimmering waters just like the sea,
go up on the mountains over the trees
to find the wolf that represents three.

Revenge and Rage
by Liam Powers

Wiping back tears, fleeing this hellscape, I take a single step
That pompous gaslighter deserves not even a speck of dust
but I must take another step
My face appears to be a waterfall; I yearn to leave;
I must augment the size of my steps
I despise that happiness thief, that moody, vain, vulgar villain.
YOU believe my feelings are a Parker Brothers board game.
Five hours later, I cry myself to sleep hugging that yellow polka-dotted pillow.
The same pillow YOU gifted me on my twentieth birthday
The following Friday, I assault it and shred it till it breaks.
I tear, and I tear till that stupid pillow gives in.
… Why won't it break; it shall meet its demise.
I want this pillow to be YOU.
I'm tired of YOU; there is only one way to end our ongoing strife.
Your existence vexes me day by day.
Why did you do this? YOU created a monster out of me
What is this? Could it be my villain origin story?
My spiral into madness, the hunger and pain
YOU inflicted on my soul on this day.
I have finally seen behind your venomous masquerade.
I'm done, I'm done; for all these years, I've stopped wiping back my tears.
I'm a phoenix from the ashes I have gotten my wings
Now I fly away from your clingy disgusting grasp.

Unify
by Isabella Porrini

Unity is something that we seek, yet we cannot find
A solution that must come together, and withstand the test of time
Something that starts with a change of heart, starts with a change of mind
When faced with a global pandemic, and there was nowhere to run
We had to work together, we had to work as one
We tried to had in harmony, and towards a common goal
Trying to solve a problem, unknowing what the future would hold
People are always judging, unable to put differences aside
Unable to respect others, refusing to even try
Impudence is shown to others with different beliefs and minds
Rather than compassion, for we are all mankind
And although it seems impossible to find an adequate solution,
We must first understand
That all people have different views
Some that don't go hand-in-hand
We must change our attitude, and take this step by step
For we have come far, it would be a shame to go back
Yet as each day passes by, there are more and more issues that arise
We must learn from the past and learn to be wise
We must come together
We must unify

Lyric Analysis
by Dalilah James

Lyrics tell stories so big that can be simplified to minutes
that leave a person in tears or joy
Radical Face's "Always Gold" tells the story of a friend looking back
on his friendship with a friend struggling with addiction
The Front Bottoms "Twin Size Mattress" shares a similar story of a friend trying
to grasp his friend struggling with an addiction while pleading with him to stay
One Republic's "I Lived" has the perspective of a father's wish for his son
to have the experience in life and live in the moment
Taylor Swift's "Long Live" is her telling the story of her success she shares
with her bandmates and fans and her wish to look back on her life
and never be forgotten. I never understood that when I was younger,
songs held a deeper meaning to them
Rob Thomas's "Little Wonders" has the impression of a father looking back
on his memories with his kids, good or bad,
had an unforgettable impact, their little wonders.
Lily Kershaw's "Ashes Like Snow" is from a perspective of a person
thinking about a friend or relative that passed on
Demi Lovato's "Sober" is a three minute-seventeen second apology to her friends
and family for no longer being sober anymore
Jennifer Lopez's "Feel the Light" shares a gentle toned song as she comforts
someone in pain. I don't believe anyone who says no song has ever had an affect
on them if you find the right song.

Mundane Serenade
by Ceirra Carter

My mind races with just mention of your name
And it even finds its way to my lips in the form of prayers every night
To see you in front of me again
I could only wish to hear your voice once more
The way it felt while my dear spoke hours on end of nothing at all
But your love was never something I could ask for, Eleanor
I have long since understood
Your inability to reciprocate my fondness for you
But still you steal my heart
While the hole in my chest remains devoid of its once rhythm,
you stand there smiling
A thousand miles across the country with it still beating in your hand
Bruised and torn as it is
You hold it close as it beats in its normal ugly pattern
Oh ... ?
My dear Eleanor holds my heart delicate still,
and I feel again what I have been missing
It was a new feeling
This time not pity
It was her empathy
Beautiful as it was like my dear, but warm
So very warm

Life's Bleak Partner
by Carolyn Sparacio

Too many a time, I have pondered demise, for me, for humanity.
Humans live off Host, unsparingly, devastating entities symbiotic.
Damp forests massive, hewed for simple plantations unnecessary.
Shadowing, black cloak accompanying large, tall blade arced.
It concludes the end, patiently striking, heart beats wanning to nought.
It will abduct the world's soul, when, after the exhaust of resources?
When my time comes, my spirit sees a world dead, reaper leads to other side.
Possibly, but a casket overpriced, incinerated ashes restricted, an ornate box.
Definitely, a constant property is death, making melancholy past loved ones.
Perhaps none are bringers of death, but one becomes cold naturally stiff.
Maybe my soul travels to final judgement, heart scaled against fluffed plumage.
How does, jackal-headed, the deity perceive pure versus evil, with such ease?
Mayhap, my spirit voyages down, across Styx, must owe ferryman the toll.
If I'm destined to the pit, know I've accidentally enraged the pantheon.
Wishing for glorious meadow, but certainly, my everlasting resting place it is not.
Or possibly I emerge to Heaven, following being accepted narrowly.
Does it present, as my imagined, wooly clouds poofy beneath suburbs familiar?
Will beloved, panther inky and lion silvery,
reunite with me, told of a bridge multicolor?
Ironic, death so certain, all afterwards mysteriously unknown.
Perhaps there's nothing, psyche evaporating to void.

The Land of the free
by Payton Kindt

America the land of the free
It's home to both you and me
Yet I look around and what do I see
I see crimson blood flood the streets
I see people scream and plea down on their knees
While the pigs on their pedestals turn their heads and say
"Shut your mouth and stay"
They say they want their children to be safe
But they're cause their kids to ache in pain
Because they've never cared, all they can do is send "Thoughts and prayers"
America the land of the "free"
They take us away in handcuffs because they don't agree
with who you are and who you'll be
They fill our throats with stuffing and beg us not to stand
Because they all want to believe that this is the "perfect" land
America the land of the "free"
But it's no longer a home
And it's no longer with me
It's a prison
And I'm gone
Because there's nowhere to call my home

I Wish To Understand Your Love
by Nino Kreider

I wish to understand love poems, but I write more than I receive.
To understand how to act when writing one, when reading one.
I wish to understand your love in a way that doesn't make me cry at its rarity.
I wish, I wish, I wish, and I give, and someone smiles
at the love I only gather from what other people think is normal.
I barely know what love is.
I want to know how not to blush, or smile,
or feel so heavily whenever love is around.
I wish to understand how not to love.
If it's false, do I walk off or drown in it because it still feels so good?
If it's wrong, do I condemn it or live my life a secret
all for the false hope of freedom I don't deserve?
If it's meant to feel like home,
do I dig myself out of this grave I've made out of your words?
Am I supposed to hear you?
Speak up, I can't recognize your voice under six feet of lies
and the coffin in which the blood of my shattered heart has stuck to and dried.
I wish to understand the love you were supposed to give me,
so I can decipher through everything else I got instead.
I wish to understand your love, I wish to understand, I wish to love, I wish.
But I never get my happy ending, and the poem stops,
and my careless wishes are never finished.

Summer Mornings
by Brigid Kelly

When you wake up in the morning
And the circular shape of the sun is forming
... Everything feels calm
You hear the sound of seagulls
While the waves are crashing
As the sand crabs are passing
You open your windows and smell the crisp morning air
The light breeze comes through and blows your hair
It's like nothing else matters
The door is opened and you enter onto your porch
The sun feels as if it's a burning torch
But you still feel just right
The summer sun, serotonin is contagious, no matter where you live.

Being
by Ellen Bennett

The power which comes from the force of a soul
Is one to not be underestimated.
The emotions that comes from the mind of a soul
Are ones raw with potential to change dramatically,
But yet, they don't
The being of a content soul
With the being they reside in as their blanket for safety
Serves a brilliant reminder that
Anyone can flourish with their concealed soul in place
A soul that feels trapped in captivity
Cannot flourish like their joyful counterparts.
A soul who feels defeated
Cannot radiate the power that their peers feel
A soul whose being feels like a prison
Cold, empty, cramped, imperfect
Cannot supply the warmth and spirit needed for their being to survive.
A soul that feels defeated
Does not have the spirit to survive.
As those souls in their beings laugh,
One soul cries
As those souls in their rightful beings dance
One soul sulks
One soul cannot progress through life
If they feel defeated
One soul whose body feels like a dreadful chamber
Cannot laugh, or sing, or dance
They are only condemned to sadness
To lost hope
Until they remember that they have the power within themselves
To change their being, and to change themselves

My Sister
by Myah Lockwood

Roses are red, violets are blue
and the sweetest lil sister I know.
Nothing will change that.
Nothing will get between us.
I've been happy since the day you were born.
When we play together it's all I could wish for.
The day I met you I was happy cuz you were so sweet.

Italian Food
by Kaylee Bachman

Oh how I love Italian food
I eat it all the time.
Not just 'cause how it good tastes
But 'cause how good it rhymes.
Minestrone, Cannelloni,
Macaroni, Rigatoni,
Spaghettini, Scallopini,
Escarole, Braciole,
Insalata, Cremolata, Manicotti,
Marinara, Carbonara,
Shrimp Francese, Bolognese,
Ravioli, Mostaccioli,
Mozzarella, Tagliatelle,
Fried Zucchini, Rollatini,
And Tetrazzini,
Oops- I think I split my Jeani.

Detached
by Anthony Sosnovskiy

Lost in a world that's not my own,
I wander through these streets alone.
The sky above, a shade too bright,
An unfamiliar world within my sight.
I try to grasp what's real and true,
But everything seems off, askew.
The faces around me, all a blur,
A distant memory, a faint whisper.
The colors, the sounds, the smells,
All distorted, like a twisted spell.
A world that once felt so concrete,
Now feels like a dream, incomplete.
I long to escape this surreal place,
To find my way back to the human race.
But for now, I'm lost in this haze,
Wondering when my reality will be ablaze.

No Peeking
by Medine Bulanadi

I never wanted to be the villain
Yet people used me in sinful ways
Making me the most biggest sin in the world
- lies

Why
by Akasha (Ace) Gaber

Lost in mind
Lost in thought
"Are you ok?"
"Yeah I'm fine ... "
Living to the eye
Dead inside
Crying to myself
In the dark of my room
wishing for hope
The sole of death
Seeps with a lie
The depths of my mind
A spiral gone insane
A toe curling pain
Spine chilling screams
Lights going out
Darkness strikes
The depth of the sick

Oranges
by Saskia Ajax

When I think of oranges
I think of a bittersweet taste
A cold and refreshing feeling
It takes me back to when I was 6
When my mother worked in the summers
And my grandmother pushed fruits on us every day
I think of peeling the skin back and making a mess of myself
I remember how I hated orange juice
Any orange flavor in all honesty
I remember how my mom's favorite colors were orange and green
But orange was never my color
Orange was never my flavor
When was orange ever the first choice
It left a sour taste in my mouth
And an ugly stain in my eyes
Just how it left a permanent mark on my soul
Now I know why I've never liked orange

The Thousandth Man
by Elizabeth McClintock

Most people will just go through the motions
Without making much of a commotion.
But the thousandth man would.
He would try and try until no one else could.
The other 999 people just try to get through the day.
The thousandth man makes the most of it and keeps his thoughts at bay.
He wants to help those around him
And make their days not grim.
People need to appreciate the thousandth man
Because without him they would have no plan.

Dove and Glove
by Lily Arnold

There was a dove
That flew from above
Until it found a glove
The glove helped it find love
When in distress the dove went to glove
They even played drums
They helped tie hair into buns
They even grew close enough to find groves
Dove and glove were there even when things got rough
Together all through the months
With dove and glove there was no rush
It was the kind of love you would find in a treasure trove
Dove started cooking with stoves
Glove started to pick mangroves
That my friends is the reminiscent of dove and glove

Carpe Diem
by Aleena Zeejah

I look up to see a crystal clear blue sky on a beautiful spring day
Look down below my feet, lie the most green grass I had ever seen
Look to my right to see nothing but pure joy and happiness
while families gather together to celebrate the day
Look to my left to see the children playing tag with each other
screaming "I'm coming!"
I sit on the ground and I look around
Missing a lot of things that I used to be able to do, see, hear, touch
But now I find gratitude in the now
Because each day is a gift that should be enjoyed to the fullest
That's why we call it the present
Because it's a reminder that each day is a gift
That we need to be grateful for everything
Because before you know it
It's all gone

Glass Doll
by Cortney Chandler

Darling put that glass doll back on the shelf
You know she'd break if she fell
Her face is cracked from crying too many tears
But her eyes are dry, for she has given up in despair
Her dress is perfect
Her hair golden like the sun
And she knows she will be trapped forever
So she never tries to run

Pain
by Alexis Tice

The pain isn't something that can be described
Only something that can be prescribed
Pain is something that's felt
It usually comes from the cards you're dealt
Pain creates a world in your head
A world where you don't go to bed
A world that keeps you from sleep
So that all you can do is weep
Pain is something you see in someone's eyes
All their lows and highs
The hurt from the lies
Though through all the pain they hold a pretty good disguise
Though every day that I am alive
Through all this pain I will survive
And every day I see the big blue sky
I know that I will get up and try

My Feathery Family
by Arianna Flores Rojas

We are a flock of birds, All different from each other
Soaring above the world in our own little cluster
The sky is our home, it is free and vast,
It is like a fairy tale, that is always going to last
As we continue on, the night rolls in
and the shimmer of stars glistens off the ocean's skin
We fly to a branch to spend the night
We huddle together nice and tight
In the morning the journey continues on
We look out for each other All day long
Finally we made it to our nest
Our journey felt like an amazing quest
Above we see the moon so bright
As if it were a giant flashlight
We preen each other to show our love
We say good night from our nest up above

The Flow
by Elizabeth Harris

Everyone always says to go with the flow and I have,
That led me down a steep waterfall,
Into shallow and fast-flowing rapids,
hitting every sharp rock in my path
Poking little holes in the side of my boat,
What's going to be next?
Are there going to be alligators with sharp long, teeth
eating piece after piece until it's all gone,
Or finally do I get to relax and go down the river
Peacefully, calmly, until the end …

Ring, Ring, Ring
by Riley Terry

Ring, Ring, Ring
That's the sound of a tired mallet
Hitting its head hard on a shiny, metallic, cylinder
It's a daily song
But this song is a total flop
The ring clones itself across the room
Yet not a soul retorts
My peers disregard the thought
Recommencing with the clatter
While my pupils chat and howl
I sit at my isolated table
Watching the chaos ensue
So even though my pupils don't know
That everytime the tired chimes cry
I become exasperated

With You
by Nicole Sandoval

Walking by the sunsets with you
Thinking of us growing old together love can have many feuds
But it can last forever
Smells of roses when she passes by
But it disappears right away
Reading is a hobby we have alike
We both have music that make us feel a certain way
Thoughts of love run into my mind
Love is pain is what people say
Love is hard to find
But, there is always a way
The way you shine
There is hope in my eyes
To see you past by
And enchanting my life

My Neighbor's Dog
by Bre Ward

His name is Dewey
He likes things that are chewy
He gets so excited to see me
Basically knocks me to my knees
I like to take him for a walk
If he sees a cat he starts to bark
Loves it when I brush his fur
He's not mine, he belongs to her
She lets me pretend he's mine
And I play with him all the time
He's my best friend
Me and Dewey till the end.

Surviving
by Charlotte Hautala

I've learned how to type without looking
I've learned how to speak French
I've learned how to read backwards
All hard skills but you know what's harder?
Surviving
Surviving is a tough skill
The world beats us and hurts us
And expects us to survive?
Some people may never know
how tough it really is
It challenges us
We face it
We live
We survive

The Platforms That Poison Our Minds
by Natalie Kuczwaj

Social media is an addiction.
It's like the nicotine in cigarettes,
just another form of self-infliction,
cause us to drown in our own regrets.
We scroll through TikTok and Snapchat all night
instead of enjoying time with our peers,
hoping to get certain numbers of likes,
and if we don't we will end up in tears.
All of a sudden we care how we're seen.
All of a sudden we must be perfect.
Social media kills our self esteem.
Put the phone down and you'll see its effect.
We still choose to keep scrolling and scrolling.
We are the ones our phones are controlling.

Stranger
by Maya Muntyan

He was a stranger
Never thought of him as anything
That all changed after a simple "hey"
We texted from "good morning" to "goodnight"
I felt a connection
I didn't know what to feel.
I felt happiness.
But also confusion
We didn't go one day without texting to each other.
Now, it's like I don't even know him
He is a stranger.

Japan
by Meya Bellmer

I can smell the cherry blossoms
Down the street and in the trees
Feel it through your bones deep inside
There are many things to make you feel like this
Fresh rain, soil, many more
You may feel like a cherry blossom
You're not understood, small, frail, weak
But lovely, graceful, powerful, different
This is why
Just like snowflakes on Mt. Fuji
All special in many ways
Like a bun in a bakery fresh
Fresh sea water on the boat
Just refreshed

Unfair
by Alexis (Lexi) Ricoy

"you sensitive, emotional thinker"
"you fragile, little girl"
they say this while pointing their crooked, grotesque finger
and when they say this, they let their stomach wrenching misogyny unfurl
you are nothing but an object, just for their self-motivated eyes
your persona must be a certain way, however, always be unique
and when you state your opinion, you'll eternally be deemed the 'bad guy'
they'll drain your mood, until you find yourself under your own gray sky
and what may these creatures be called?
the ones that chase, objectify, and harass in clans
one can wonder, if they're even human at all
for this unsettling species, is the species of man
so when you encounter them, do proceed with care
for this is the unfortunate life of a woman, which is irrevocably unfair

My Last Breath
by Alec Autry

I hope my last breath is a sigh of relief,
Not one pain,
Not one of grief,
But one of love and one of peace.
With each exhale, I let it go,
The stress and strain that brought me low.
May I find joy in the arms of the divine,
And leave this world with a content mind.
With no worries to hold me back,
My burdened heart finally gets to relax.
May my soul soar high above,
Embraces by pure and endless love.

My Heart Belongs To History
by Trinity Chavez

My love for you is deep
Deeper than can be
You taught right from wrong
So I will sing your song
You proved time and time again
That we are Americans
You showed us wars and dark times
But I'll take it as mine
You showed us racism and poverty
But you have also showed us liberty
Which is why my heart is yours
I left it for you at the door
I love you so History
You are my lovey mystery

Illuminate My Sky
by Angelina Triantafillis

Golden twins pulled apart by the force of a god.
The winds of freedom washing over his emptiness,
The golden and red leaves lay on mountains
made by his spears of law and contract,
Thunderous fiery in part of her destined eternity,
Books stacked high of wisdom growing into insanity like the tree she grew,
Blue waters carrying justice for her jester,
Raging fires evolved from her war and passion,
The loving pierce of an icicle in the coldest winters caring for her children,
A forgotten nation only to be found in words.
The crystal and stone woman in the sky watching down on my every step.
A demented world or dimension I never wanted to happen.
I've lost my individuality and my sister to gods.

The Letter Never Sent
by Giselle T. Letren

Found in an old journal, I used to keep
I found a letter, a letter never sent.
I poured all my feelings into this letter
Was there a purpose? A motive for such heartbreak?
This letter was never spoken of, but ignored.
What would happen?
What would've happened if that letter WAS sent?
Would things be different? Better for us?
Would we talk about things? Make up? Fight?
The questions that raced in my mind, all because of a letter never sent.

The Bridesmaid
by Siya Evitt

Always the bridesmaid, never the bride, they say.
You feel like they're right, you cannot fight,
Watching her walk down the aisle in her pretty dress
Feeling like you're just second best.
They say, "You need to give up, give it a rest."
And so you do.
It hurts it does,
It stings and smarts,
It feels like your heart is being stabbed by darts.
Over and over again.
But you do it all for your friends.
Always the bridesmaid, never the bride.

Cycle
by Mylee Petela

One day my mother hit a skunk driving down the road
I didn't see it, but I can remember how it felt
I want to die with purpose
To become a part of the earth
More than a memory or a feeling
When I slowly decompose my skin will melt from my teeth
I'll smile without thinking
I'll make a wish in the stars that made us
To let me give myself to the ocean
So over and over
I may be experienced
Beautiful waves in the ocean, washed up
Sucked into the ground
Decomposing other things once alive
Evaporated
And elated to do it again and again
Until the death of the universe
I'd be smiling

Courage
by Chanel Wallis

I dance in the starlight, so fresh, so new,
So unafraid of what I had once led askew.
I chuckle to myself as I remember the past,
And at how naive I was to think it would last.
That's when you find me, happy and loved, as you ask why,
I can only respond then by smiling and looking you in the eye.
You startle, you gasp and nearly faint, but alas!
I catch you and hug you; my joy too wonderous for anyone to grasp.

Farming
by Draven Ferch

I love to farm and ranch with Pappy.
Driving the combine is fun.
I hate when the tractor runs out of gas.
I love to drive the semi.
I hate when the header teeth break.
I like to run fast right next to the combine.
Rider bulls are fun and dangerous.
I like to ride the horses to gather the cows.
When I'm in the combine I like to listen to country music.
I love when we brand the calves.
I love when we're done branding; we eat at the Longhorn.
I love when we race the four wheelers.

In the Realm of Imagination
by Amoya Ellis

In the realm of imagination, I am free
Boundless possibilities, without any fee
A place where I can be whoever I please
With no borders, no boundaries, and no disease.
I can soar among the clouds in the sky
Or dive with dolphins in the sea nearby
I can climb the highest mountain peak
Or explore the depths of the ocean's mystique.
My imagination is my sanctuary
A place where I can be extraordinary
And bring to life all that I see
In a world where I am truly free.
So let your imagination run wild
Like a curious, adventurous child
Explore the endless possibilities
Of a world within your mind's capacities.
In this realm of the mind's creation
You can find true liberation
And discover a world that's new
Where the only limit is you.

Nature
by D'lila Thompson

The little red and white box that stays on the desk
The mixed emotions that I'm feeling while looking at the box
Why? How was I so naive?
I need to open that box
The floorboard creaking while approaching the desk
The lock click
Standing with a blank face
The little red and white box that stays on the desk

My Father
by Jasmin Abarca-Holbrook

My father,
I do love that man
But I think only for the sole purpose of him being my father.
Because of that stupid title, I still have to wake up every day
and still love him. Or at least pretend to.
And I don't think it's fair to love someone who left all those gaps in my childhood
Why should I have to love someone who left?
Or who constantly made my mother cry?
Whose presence made my siblings and I grow up walking on eggshells?
Wondering when he would show up?
Why should I have to love someone who never felt like home?
Someone whom I've never even known?

Exceptions
by Kennedy Cranson

Judgment filling my head all-day.
Many opinions. Hard to obey.
Failure never has been an option.
Making decisions is my toxin.
Never fully pleased.
Muscle gain is what sports require.
When catching a boy, that backfires.
Left pals on open, feeling alone.
Parents keep yelling get off your phone!
Never fully pleased.
Wanting to fail no-one is my fight.
Finding myself pushing through in spite.
Learning that people are fickle;
Having two faces like a nickel.
Never fully pleased.
Finding comfort in a changeless God.
Showing his mercy and love abroad
Knowing I can't make it on my own,
He sends Jesus down from his great throne.
Never fully alone.

Juliet: Not For Me
by Nicoletta Kenney

Juliet, you're not for me, don't thou see,
We're over now, 'twas never meant to be.
Our love, like glass, too fragile, now broken.
Aphrodite blesses us not, a pity.
Cupid's arrows passed, they whizzed right past me.
Wilt I love again, with thy face present?
How can I, when thou art still existent?
And well, Juliet, thou art so ugly.
Cursed by thy mother, to look so ghastly.
Thy looks could kill, doomed for solitude,
For no man shall ever look, and love thee.

Open Up
by Noam Blumenthal

I am a sunflower, all shriveled and weak,
oh rain, oh won't you peek?
I am a rose, scarlet and beautiful,
thorns sharp, not dull.
I am a dandelion, pale and white,
I get blown away, each day.
I am a tulip, rich and vibrant,
although when I'm not cared for,
I become dry and silent.
I am a budding flower with great color and tone,
but do you know what it's like not to be shown?

My Friends and I
by Keylon Kittleson

I really like to play basketball
My friends and I even play in the hall.
We took the Tesla and landed on Mars.
Never knew we could make it this far.
Never had much food on our dishes.
We always wished for the riches.
We can play in the cold weather.
We all want to go to space.
We left this world without a trace.
My friends and I move with a passion.
We aren't moving backwards like Michael Jackson,
But we're moving forwards.
So, all the haters have no words.
Jackson, Jakai and I like to rap,
When we're on the flow, we always snap.
You got me off the beat,
Jackson and Jakai with the heat.
We are so great, you can't even compete.

Spring
by Sophia Tellason

I hear the sound of birds eating from the trees.
A cool breeze comes along.
The sweet smell of lilies soothes my mind.
As I walk along the field I enjoy the fresh air.
I feel the sun shining on my skin.
What I love the most are the flowers around me.

Mantra
by Payton Becker

I am calm, I am focused, and I am going to give 100%.
3rd set, game point, my serve, mind focused, nervous shakes, high toss–
I am calm, I am focused, and I am going to give 100%.
Final test, big grade, need an A, pencil sharp, studied hard–the paper hits the desk.
I am calm, I am focused, and I am going to give 100%.
Walk in, look around, no familiar faces, deep breath, shake my hands,
one foot in front of the other–
I am calm, I am focused, and I am going to give 100%.
Breathing fast, hands shake–I need to move.
No reason to be anxious, mind is everywhere–it will end.
I am calm, I am focused, and I am going to give 100%.
Mom is sick. No one told me. I hear the news, trust in God. It will get better.
I am calm, I am focused, and I am going to give 100%.

My Funny Eyed, Skew Jawed, Ballerina Feet
by Hannah Strümpher

Oh my funny eyed, skew jawed, ballerina feet.
You know really sometimes you can be sweet.
Your tail bangs against the doors
as you stumble around on all fours.
With your front feet turned outward
and your bottom tooth sticking forward.
Oh my funny eyed, skew jawed, ballerina feet.
How you make me feel complete.
Your bark echoes for everyone to hear
always with one out turned ear.
Your blue jersey as you run in the snow
When you cuddle me I love you so.
Oh my funny eyed, skew jawed, ballerina feet.
How you race to be the first to eat.
But you still don't feel satisfied
and when I eat you give me puppy eyes
Your nose pops out under the blanket you snuggle
How your goofy face just makes me chuckle.
Oh my funny eyed, skew jawed, ballerina feet.
Without you I am incomplete.

Inside and Out
by Kelsea Noyes

Kind heart is what people see.
Energetic and happy is what they expect.
Loving and respectful is what they deserve.
Shy and insecure is how I feel.
Easily embarrassed is how it goes.
And overthinking hurts the most.

The Un-Perfection
by Alexia Castaneda

The pitter patter of the rain
The shadows of the street lamps
The sounds of cars day and night
They have a purpose
But what's mine?
The constant portrait of perfection is never done being painted
There is always a new standard, trend or validation
Nothing stays the same
But perfection can only be imagined
There is no perfect man or woman, or happily ever after
There is only you, them and the world
They say you only live once, but it's a lie
You die once but you live every day.

Flowers
by Dahfna Katzenberg

I smell flower
Beautiful, dainty flowers
With their soft and silky petals
And the dust of pollen collecting on my fingers.
When I smell flower
I am happy
As their beauty transcends the universe
"But" you may say,
"You never mentioned seeing them."
To that I say elegance and beauty don't matter
When something like a flower exists
They can be seen by the gifted
They can be looked upon and loved for their beauty
But flowers are more than just beauty
They have meanings, symbolisms
You can give flowers to a person and hear how happy they are.
But flowers don't last forever
Yet it is still courteous to enjoy them
You may see them while I can't
But I'm still happy.

The Walk
by Hayven Romero

There are many things
The Walk can be.
The Walk of Shame,
Possibly.
The Walk of Pride,
Just maybe.
The Walk can be
Many things.
Like a natural evening stroll
Or a sentiment in the mind.
The Walk is like an emotion
The Walk can feel feelings
Like any person can.
The Walk is usually seen
Next to something.
The Walk of Honesty
The Walk of Wonder
The Walk of Knowledge
The Walk of Life
The Walk of You.

Seasonal Friend
by Kelysha Linton

The rain is my friend
It visits from time to time
It knocks on my windows repeatedly
The rhythm calms my mind
It asks me if I'm okay
A simple question so profound
It mostly visits when I'm lonely
So I tell it I'm feeling down
It rarely visits when I'm happy
So those days are the best
They fill me with such joy
I think I must be blessed
Oh, how lucky I am
To have a forever caring friend
One who I know won't leave me
Even if it was given money to spend
Even if it may seem weird
Being friends with the rain just seems right
So I wait patiently each moment
For the day we reunite

Betrayal
by Acoya Bartlett

I love helping friends,
But no matter what
Friendships still end.
Stabs in the gut.
Because of betrayal.
I help them fight.
I help them through it.
My back they smite.
I just feel split.
Because of betrayal.
Emotions bring scars.
Hard to trust someone.
I stare at stars.
My mind is spun.
Because of betrayal.
Now I am closed off.
Emotions all gone.
Now I just scoff
When friends bring dawn.
There will come betrayal.

Glass Bottle
by Kyla Curton

The glass bottle is thrown,
thrown over a ledge
to the ground below
one little crack no one can see
But that one crack,
becomes many more
spreading like wildfire
across the entirety of it
The glass bottle sits
forever alone
The crack growing,
silently but surely
Occasionally someone will come
they'll pick it up in their arms,
most leave but there's a small group
that stays sitting around it
Though they are there,
the crack is still spreading
almost engulfing it until one day,
it shatters.

Imperfection
by Charlee Buhrle

All she does with her body is reject
She can feel her heart sink down to her toes
All she wants is to look picture perfect
She wants her skin to just shimmer and glow
So over her body being imperfect
She knows that her body is a reject
If only her body could just say whoa
If only she was not viewed an object
She wishes she was the girl in the show
Her body is nothing but imperfect
As always her body is a project
She doesn't have that pretty sunglow
She desires to see her beautiful reflect
Noticing that her body overflows
She realized her body is not imperfect
Now she knows her body is perfect
There is no more a reflected scarecrow
So now her body has some self-respect
No more an act in the circus sideshow
Her body is everything but imperfect

Healing Has No Time Frame
by Asha Soto

If there's one thing I've learned, it is that healing has no time frame,
everyone heals in different ways.
It's quite all right to miss the person you once loved every day
even if it has been three years and two days.
When you love someone,
sometimes there will be no definite end.
Sometimes their presence will still find a way to infiltrate your hear.
You'll come to hate the way the thought of them so easily pervades your head
and you'll find you still turn your hear when their scent fills the air,
you still turn your head even when you know they're not there.
But one day you'll breathe in again, and their scent will permeate your brain,
flooding your mind with the memories of you and them.
And you won't turn your head, your love for them will be just that.
A memory,
A thought,
A once was what will never be again.
And you will exhale.
Whether or not you've thought about them today,
just know that someday,
someday, the thought of them will go away.

The Ending I Needed
by Maddison Holmes

I shouldn't have fallen so fast
In my defense I thought it would last
Over and over you promised
Yet over and over you were dishonest
I don't remember why I fell
Though I will always remember our farewell
Even if this feeling lasts forever
The bond we made will always be severed
I will not give in
For if I do you will win
I cannot let that happen
Due to our bond having blackened
When the necklaces we wore snapped
So to did the bond of love we backed
You were not right in our bond being love
For all along I felt shoved
I recall every moment you were the center
Even when I tried to enter
I said goodbye and I'll say it again
This is our end

My Sorries For the One Unable To Bear a Child
by Anaiah Missouri

I'm sorry for all of your scars,
For each broken piece of your heart,
For every stillbirth you endured alone, and
Every doctor's visit hoping he had grown.
I'm sorry you never got to see his twinkling eyes, and
For every string of compromise you made for the betterment of others.
Your secret sadness never spoken aloud,
Each time you get up things keep bringing you down.
Dark spaces in your empty womb,
Passing every pregnant woman, is
Just another painful reminder of what is no longer there.
You try and deny,
Bargain and cry,
Soon accepting and repeating the cycle.
And although I will never fully understand
This thing demanding all your sorrows and misery,
But, most of all,
I'm sorry you never got to see it as a gift
The gift of patience and humility
The gift of healing and sympathy.

A New Era
by Pranav Narayanan

Where our Ancestors looked up to the sky
We stare down at our screens,
We turned learning into Snap Streaks and Discord Pings
A moment frozen,
The Instagram Reels and Tiktoks
Gone for a second,
A second of silence
Of peace,
A place of serenity
Turned dark,
Fueled only by plight, addiction, and suffering.
There is a Child
Age 6,
Bright smile and bubbly personality
Lost in a room filled with bright lights and colors,
Eyes fixated on a phone with a sparkly case
The phone slips,
It shatters his life
A lone tear runs down his face,
Then back to raising his snap score.

Being a Teenager
by Meg Thornton

Oh, being a teenager seems like so much fun,
when you're just a kid, so young, so dumb.
Just hanging out with friends, in the warm summer sun,
But once you become one you realize, life has just begun.
When you're a kid all you want to do is grow up,
but once you do, you want nothing more than to be unstuck.
To go back to playing and drinking from your cartoon cup,
Because when you're a teen, your standards go way up.
When you get into high school, it's nothing but stress,
your time for fun becomes less and less.
You have to keep pushing yourself, hoping to progress,
when all you do is try to impress.
It's not just school but everything else too,
from all of your friend's drama, to the peer pressure you endure.
They all say that they get it, they where a teenager once too,
But parents don't understand what you're going through.
It was different for them in their day and age,
they didn't have social media, that was all the rage.
They don't get that being a teen is like being on stage,
all eyes on us, expecting us to be perfect at such a young age.

The Woodlands
by Arthur Canaes

Windy woodland
A tiny rabbit springs
Across a tiny pond

In Some Classrooms
by Rigdhen Khyungra

I sit near the front.
Keylon and I shadow box.
We throw our pencils.

Move Forward But Never Move On
by Mary Grace Hagen

My body bleeds red blood from an open wound that will never close
Try and try to patch it up but this wound is too deep to heal
So difficult to keep moving when the pain rips through your mind,
your thoughts, your heart, your soul
A piece of me is lost and will never return
Keep moving forward but never move on

The Monsters In the Mirror
by Charlotte Preall

The monsters in the mirror pull at my skin,
Tear at my hair, rip at my limbs.
They steal my soul and distort my vision,
Infecting my sight with blotches of crimson.
Their hands, gnarled and spindly, cradle my face-
Whispering poisons disguised in lace.
My tears burn down my cheeks while they brush them away,
Saying "it's only your fault you're this way"
"It's okay though, we'll fix you, that's what we do"
"Just surrender to us, we'll take care of you"
They promise me love, except love at what cost-
A spirit crushed, an identity lost?
But their voices are alluring, so toxic yet pretty
I have no choice but to listen. I let them twist me.
When their work is done, I no longer exist
They leave me in pieces, scattered, adrift
I am broken, empty, completely alone
All but the monsters in the mirror, they will never be gone.

My Future
by Vincent Feliciano

The league is my dream
Shaking the commissioner's hand
One day my name on the screen

Dogs Make Good Friends
by Dakota Best

Dogs are our best friends.
Dogs play catch.
Dogs make you laugh.
Dogs put warmth in our hearts.
Dogs make you mad.
Dogs also make you glad.
Dogs are good house pets.
Dogs can be aggressive.
Dogs can be calm.
Dogs chase their tail.
Dogs like walks.
Some dogs like water.
Dogs are dogs.

Validation
by Thalya Shupe-Ruiz

Validation is everything
My energy I put
I don't know where it goes
I was told I was special
By teachers and adults alike
The praise I got for being smart
Shattered into a million pieces
For I am not special or smart
Disappointed by life and trail
For if I wasn't told I was special
Maybe I wouldn't be hurt
Academic Validation you are gone
I cry at night stressed
For my plate is too full
Ready to cave in
But I still strive for
Academic Validation
No matter how much I
Bleed, suffer, and cry
I refuse to cave

Haiku
by Emery Nunn

I can't count at all.
Syllables are very hard.
It is upsetting.

Dear End
by Sophie Chirila

The bomb stopped ticking.
Everyone stood silently,
Waiting for death's hands.

The Wise Teacher
by Joseph LaDelfa

A beacon of light
Patiently guiding my path
Teacher, wise and young

Life
by Lance Markstaller

Life can be beautiful
It can also be bountiful
Life can be depressing
Life can also be oppressing
Life can be liberating
Life can also be berating
In life you can be victorious
In life you can be inglorious
Life can be destructive
Life can be productive
Life can be joyful
Life can be like a foible
Life can be disabling
It can also be stabling
Life can be enjoyable
Life can be deployable
Life can be for accomplishments
Life can be also full of unaccomplishment
Life is good
Life can be understood

3rd Place

Ava Meisel

Hearts On the Pavement
by Ava Meisel

Sitting on the warm pavement
Drawing hearts with our chalk
Leaving a rosy dust on our hands
Over us a lilac tree stands tall full of life
The brisk wind sending a wonderful scent our way
As time goes on the chalk fades,
Disappearing slowly
Along with the lilac tree once full of life, now lifeless,
The lilac scent now nonexistent
I draw more hearts hoping for them to reappear
As vibrant as they were before
But the vacant look in your eyes tells me that
Although the hearts we drew will never completely disappear
They will be forever
Faded.

2nd Place

Rory Neilson

Warm Sunny Days
by Rory Neilson

As the last package is boxed
And the rumbling, rickety truck pulls away
We chase it, our bare feet hitting rocks.
We run together, breathing heavily
Stopping at the end of the street
Hugging each other on the last day
I whisper into your ear, so quietly no one else hears
Remember
Remember the summer days together
As we sat together under the sprinklers
That were meant for the blooming flowers
Remember the dogs, barking in the night
Keeping us awake as we watched for shooting stars
Lighting up the entire night sky
But only for a second
So short that if I blinked, it would be gone
But still there, in the sky, just on a different planet
And like those stars,
I know you are still there, somewhere,
Remembering those warm, summer days

1st
Place

Kaylan Gagnon

A competitive gymnast,
Kaylan wrote this $100 award-winning poem
while in the eighth grade.
A labor of love, "The Key" is a tribute to a great grandmother
who had a wonderfully positive influence
in the early life of this young poet!
Thank you, Kaylan!

The Key
by Kaylan Gagnon

We play a game,
me and my grandmother
a game of wonder
in my hopeful eyes.
She hides the key,
harder and harder to find each time.
If I found it,
it would come home with me
and then come back the next time.
I always hoped
one day that clever key
would come home with me for good.
One tragic-unexpected day
that key did come home with me.
I did not want the key anymore.
It hurt
to know that that wonderful
and hopeful key that it once was in my eyes,
has turned into a symbol of loss.

Division IV

Grades
10-12

Holding Peace
by Cassandra Boislard

Silence fills the room
as the officiant asks for objections to be announced or forgotten.
The Groom stares into the crowd of faces,
as his eyes fall upon the young man in the crowd, his expression begins to soften.
The young man's mouth remains closed, as if it was sewn shut.
His eyes filled with sadness and pain.
For they both know that their objections would all be in vain.
The love they share is not to be taken seriously,
the young man must give up his feelings for the Groom.
Their love will collect dust as if it was enclosed in a tomb.
As the couple kiss, the bride's heart swells with bliss.
The young man's heart shatters, as he begins to feel amiss.
The Groom begins to doubt as he starts to reminisce.
The young man begins to weep.
The love he holds for the Groom begins to fall in a heap.
The others believe it to be joy for the newlyweds.
But the salty tears come from pain.
All these feelings the young man is expected to contain.
Hundreds of moments all in vain.

The Cherry Tree
by Elias Michael

Behind the cherry tree so fair,
I saw an eye that gave a scare,
A frightening orb, transparent and bright,
It pierced my soul, gave me a fright.
It watched me closely, never blinking,
With a gaze so intense, it left me thinking,
What secrets did it keep within,
What horrors lurked behind that skin.
I felt its power, its eerie might,
As it followed me through the night,
Its presence lingered, a haunting ghost,
A reminder of what I feared the most.
But in the daylight, I returned to see,
The cherry tree in all its majesty,
And though the eye still watched from behind,
I found solace in what I could find.
For beauty and terror can coexist,
And sometimes, it's the things we resist,
That hold the key to unlocking our fears,
And help us see past the tears.
So I embrace that terrifying eye,
And the cherry tree beneath the sky,
For in their union, I find a truth,
That sometimes beauty is in the uncouth.

Slave To Reality
by Oba-ara Fashakin

Slave of Reality
Who Lives? Who Dies? Who decides?
I am a Slave of Reality
I was born to testify against the immorality
Of this world that fosters
the original sin we wear as a cloak
the same reality in the shadow of a benevolent God
yet despite the presence of He that abides within,
we are painted in Evil ...
We bear witness to the sin we use
to procreate life into what seems to be a condemned world
cloaked in the stains of this world
wearing sin like a magnificent garment
yet it masks us in its infinite blemishes
laying amongst the very producers
of this world's filth
We who contaminate it
face inevitable judgment as mortals
yet a significant portion of our species
can wake up with smiles on their faces and filled with joy
from the blooming of a spring flower and put faith
in One unseen to the eye but sensed by the heart

What I Don't Know
by Giovanna Diehl Milisic

There's so much I can't know about the cogs that keep the universe turning,
Why a wind blow creates a chime,
And a wick keeps the fire burning.
I sometimes try to contemplate,
Still as rain and meditate,
On the genius of the architect
Creating the world, to keep it in check
But as I spend my time to worry my warts
And furrow my brow over how
I can create a change that I can't arrange
I forget the things I know:
I know the squeezes like embers of a fire
I know the giggles like tweety-birds singing
I know the eye rolls, you call me a "sigher"
I know the sharing of clothes, the "twinning"
I don't need to know why the ocean crashes
Why evil words are dished in lashes
Leaving scars that won't be healed
When I come home and it's love I feel
The love that radiates from you to me like the sun
Growing the vines of my heart, grabbing you, and we're one.

Nani
by Rachna Singh

Nani means grandmother.
Nani means vermillion stained hair and home-cooked halwa
The halwa she feeds me as she teaches me the times table;
And as shows me her intelligence that she never fully exposed to the world.
As her red glass clinks in a melodic tune,
The bangles that adorn her wrists create a beat in rhythm with her walk.
She walks on golden toe rings filled with gems
Wrapped in a patterned chiffon saree
"Rani beti" she says,
Her voice sweet and soft
As she hands me ginger chai
Freshly brewed
Her hands work like magic
It feels like sunlight and a fresh tea river
Warm like her homemade sweaters
Rich like her love for me
"Lovely daughter" she says,
In the mother tongue,
As she braids my hair with her darling hands.
Nani is the memory of my beautiful past
and the light that guides me to my future path.

Playing Catch Up
by Alexa Montano

It's the same, it's the same each and every day
Learn, know, write, and show then come home and again learn, know, write, show
Go to bed at 2 AM then do it all over again it is always the same
The same people, the same classes, the only new thing is the shape of my glasses
The same bells, the same work, the same struggling in classes
The same struggling to do better, but failing the classes.
The same late nights, but my results are never passive.
Can't they see, can't they hear, why does everyone feel blind here
Can't they see my tired eyes, can't they hear my sorrowed cries
I tell them that I need their help, but they turn away and I just yelp.
Can't you see, can't you hear, I'm so very tired, and life is getting harder here.
People call me dumb and stupid, but I never wanted to do this,
People like to say I'm slow, but don't realize how much it brings me below.
People like to call me S.P.E.D. but really
don't understand what goes on in my head
I try my hardest and barely succeed
I'm happy for my C even when they don't believe in me
But now I sit here in this class full of empty faces
Thinking of living as if life and I were in two different places
Remembering that this is just the beginning, and this is how it is going to be
Everything I say and write is in variety,
If this is true for you to know it's not just you.

Another Tragedy Cloaks the Week
by Emily Scherl

A solemn voice tells us to stand for the Pledge,
Then to stay standing to mourn the too-young dead.
We're promised justice,
But too many teachers and students are dead from a plague they won't stop.
Sobbed pleas for safety float unnoticed like dandelion seeds,
And holy #@*& I am ANGRY.
The big men in suits don't act like it's a big deal,
so my life must not be worth more than the gun lobby.
If my life feels destined to become a harrowing statistic,
Then someone is failing me.
I am resigned to panic and anger because it is all I know,
Quietly planning how I would escape the drill to end all drills.
I hear my father's voice waver,
And it's subtle but devastating.
I've only ever heard him cry for dead family,
And I think that's what's happening;
He sees my sister and I in those kids,
And I don't think he's wrong.
It could have just as easily been us.
Stop letting us wait to be next.

Four Years Later
by Daniela Parmigiani

They say high school is the best four years of your life.
They say those four years will go by in the blink of an eye.
Yet I sit here staring at the minute hand that drags behind the second hand
and wondering when I get to go home.
Wondering when my homework will be done.
Wondering when I get to go to sleep.
Wondering when my life won't consist of the same cycle every week.
Wake up. Go to school. Go to dance. Homework. Sleep. Repeat.
I wake up every day hoping for adventure only to fall asleep disappointed
that I lived out the same day that I did yesterday.
And the day before that. And the day before that.
So if high school is going to fly by,
then why won't the minute hand move faster.
In retrospect, time has moved rather quickly.
I'm left with a typical four years of high school.
Four years filled with boyfriends and parties.
Confusion and judgment.
Betrayal and jealousy.
Aspirations and goals.
High expectations.
Four years filled with unanswered questions
and a mind that continues to ask more.
Who are "they" and when did "they" make such a verisimilar statement?

Red
by Jade Alexander

Red is a color of anger
Anger is a feeling of betrayal or dishonesty
Red is a color for rage
Rage gives you a feeling way more worse than anger
Red is a color for anger and rage
All different colors can mean all different emotions for some people
Red

Songbird
by Emilia Adsuar

Songbird, why do you call so early?
I am swelled and swooned by stone fruit
Soul juice
Voices of spring burrow my hands in soil
sire sugar that cakes my teeth
Sweet tea
Sour lemon
the fat raccoon stole the crowns of my sunflower stem
Time and time again
He told me to leave the roots
Without them, the songbirds cannot make their measures
It is important that they compose
Songbird, why do you call so early?
all the great tall trees, grass, and weeds have been growing too fast
Too many measures to make
So the songbirds must call early

Plans For a Sweet 16
by Bianca Zou

During the 3rd season of every year, my Dad takes me
fishing. I swing my rod aimlessly into the moving
ocean. He asks if I'm seasick; I lie, clearly shutting
my eyes and trying not to throw up with every light
rocking. Even on land, my tan skin still reeks of
fish. Specks of pollen ache to be let into my mind and
sore body, as sticky pressure builds inside. My family gathers to
celebrate my birthday. My Dad then asks if I knew how much he
loved me. But after I finished eating the fish that was forced onto my plate,
sometimes I'd dream of a hug. His gift to me would be a hug
and eating my melting ice cream cake. He would squeeze his
eyes and twist his tongue, making it was taste like Chinese Matcha
cake that he would slice on his special day. But I know it is the pollen speaking.
The wind blew it up into the sky, forming a tall man too skinny for his
age. The grains communicated to form a small girl, straight black hair. The
two embrace, the pollen now warm and bright from their body heat.
Then a tiny flutter of wind blew past and I was left alone again.

Spring
by Taylor Uhing

The crisp air lingers through the long and frigid night
But sun could wipe the cold from the world
Owls begin laying their bold voices to rest
While doves fill the wind with coos
Nocturnal hunters retreat to their dens
Their prey living another day
Trees embrace new leaves
Grass turns green
Wildflowers bloom
Spring

Daisy
by Dakota Wiesner

A Daisy grew in a field of yellow Lilies
Not knowing of anything but rusted Red Roses
She wandered the soil and came upon the smooth sand of the desert
Until the rain began to pour, leaving the road decomposed
She longed for the deep shade of red that only Chrysanthemums could carry
But Instead she turned Yellow by liquid Aloe
All the Honeysuckle and Blue Violet got washed away
However, new flowers grew the next day
Even though it wasn't what she wanted, Spring eventually appeared
She valued knowing the Goldenrods and their various ways
Then be completely drowned out by the flood
All she desired was to be red
But she became a white chrysanthemum instead
Without even noticing that the Daisy in her was already dead

Current
by Seth Allhiser

As I gazed into the clear water
I saw silvery fish swimming in the beaver pond
The water in the pond was slower and hotter
Then a new thought dawned
I realized the fish in the creek were us
The fish in the current frantically try to stay in place
The fish in the current get stronger from swimming in a race
These fish never seem to care and would never fuss
The fish in the pool are weaker and more carefree
As the beaver dam rots away, what will disappear is their glee
The weaker fish will struggle as their sanctuary is now just debris
This is true with humans as well
The people raised in the hands of difficulty are stronger
They delight in the sound of rushing gurgling water crashing rocks while it fell
They know this is when progress and change are in their hands for longer
Those raised weak will fall as the babbling brook of life grows in its intensity

Home
by Carly Germano

There's always something about the mountains
It makes the trees look like spewing fountains
But the sky is the star of the show
It makes my perspective grow
I love the water
It looks like a beautiful daughter

Why Lord?
by Alivia Fine

Innocence lost trying to find it again she cries, Lord help
Her words are lost she can't pray so she calls, Lord help
Lost in tears and pain waiting for answers she asks, Lord help
Forgiveness and forgetness she stops asking, Lord help
Slowly she breaks into the world and lives her life
Broken again she breathes, Lord help
Again and again only able to breathe the words, Lord help me ... please?
Death close and all alone she screams, Lord help
Love finds her and breathes life into her, thank you Lord
Scared and hurting with burdens on her soul, Lord help
Insomnia pain to many tears fallen, Lord help
Suffocating air jumping out from her lungs, Please
Hope and fear, Lord help
Finally, she asks the question
Why Lord?
No answer.

There Is No Such Thing As Perfection
by Khushi Talluru

To win, to lose
It is everything but a muse.
This competition may seem like nothing, but to me,
The thought of defeat is crushing.
The smell and the taste of validation are so near
Yet it is anything but clear.
Maybe if I try harder
Maybe if I pull more all-nighters.
I'll seem like such a brave fighter.
But all the hard work will be for naught.
For once again, I will be defeated with another loss.
Is it pointless to try?
After all this, I say no.
Because there is no such thing as losing, only giving up.
And though it may not seem like it, every opportunity is another chance
To advance your skills and practice
And remember, take it easy on yourself,
because there is no such thing as perfection.

Welding
by Brennan Marsh

I am a welder
Welding is so fun
Welding is not boring
It is second to none
Welding takes practice
It takes time and skill
This is my dream job
And it should pay more than just one bill

06/24/22
by Stella Van Buskirk

good morning, america. we're screwed.
wake up to find out that you're unloved.
most days don't live in infamy, but this one will.
this one will kill like a mockingbird.
this one made four people on a rooftop quiet.
mourn the fourth of july with us. mourn the women and the children.
We'll rest our feet in the genesis of this hate.
it's not our fault. it's not our fault we're angry.
how can there be a hero at a time like this?
there are fireworks in the distance, but we can't see what doesn't exist for us.
what is independence day to a woman? what is it to those shot dead?
hear a bell toll for every ex-freedom.
scratch your name someplace permanent before you can't anymore.
here we are. ankle deep in a mud so vicious.
who will save us now?

Nature You
by Lillian Noon

You are an infant sprout, trembling in Wind
You are first taste of Rain, humid scent laying heavy over molten roads
You are sour bitter taste of vulnerable hurt, copper tang in veins
That wrap me in cotton love
There is a soft warmth in the empty space of your hands
You are that echoing SNAP of broken bones and that slow dull healing ache
You are nervous fire flight electricity shooting off
and bringing color to tied tongues
Beautiful, oh, Beautiful. Breathless in the escapes and crests of salted waves
Emotion and brine crashing
Erosion
Aged and Etched in the stone of white bone
You are the silence in the loud clash of life
The stillness in a scream
And that peace after war.
You are the decay
The divinity and mortality of an infant sprout

Through My Imagination
by Hailey Donner

Believing in things that were never really there
Or the ability to touch when there's nothing but air
Having color and stars bleeding into every corner of my mind
Or making castles in the clouds while gazing at the sky
My brain is a vivid world apart from our own
And it focuses on things that others are seldom shown
My fictional thoughts seep into my reality
And it changes the way I see things and my mentality
But at the end of the day after taking in more of God's creation
I realize one of my favorite things he made is my imagination

Caged
by Olivia Tyson

For oh so long I've longed to be set free,
The burning need is all encompassing.
I'm scared of what they've created for me,
my waiting is coming to a closing.
I wish I could escape this mind made cage,
The cage I am trapped in day after day.
My internal sanity hard to gage,
As they control smoke blocking my airway.
I wish I had made much better choices,
Maybe I wouldn't be in this big mess.
I'm getting tired of the low voices,
But I'm crippled with the need to impress.
I am in a cage of my creation,
That will likely lead to my damnation.

Push Beyond Limits
by Paul Clement

In order to be the best version of yourself,
You must work hard and strive for greatness
Push beyond your limits
never be afraid to fail.
It's when you push hard and fight
That's when you find what you are made of
The tenacity and bravery the brain contains
Is more than enough to reach for the stars
When it gets tough
When the journey feels too long
Dig deep and find a way to keep going
Prove to yourself that you can do anything
It's through hard work and dedication
Pushing beyond your fears
That we become the best versions of ourselves
And conquer all of life's frontiers.

Glistening Ripples
by Tehya Graham

Waves roll on the sea
Down below swish its long tail
Hidden from the view
Fish swim by in schools
The orange tail moves quickly
Down to the blue pool
The light caresses
The creature underneath it
The moon rises soon

Hycinthia
by Ava Sperber

I took a rose from the vase on the counter
And trudged through the snow
To the grave of my beloved cat.
I set my rose before her cross
And stayed there for a while,
Crouched over the frost.
I must have been waiting for something.
Some sense of supernatural clarity.
Perhaps a momentary state of inner peace.
An all-consuming grief
Or a spiritual awakening.
Just a glimpse into enlightenment.
But there was nothing.
Nothing but a girl in the snow
Looking down at her dead cat's grave.

When I Write Where Do I Go?
by Taylor Anderson

When I write where do I go?
I really do not know, my mind is cloudy, like blank, white snow,
not a single thought need cross my mind,
for the words I write come from deeper inside,
no matter what it is I can attempt,
to effortlessly write, a piece of literature.
No words in my brain, just the stuff that I feel
I'm lost in a trance, when paper hits pencil, pencil hits hand,
and It's not until I get my feelings all on paper,
that I can truly understand, the words they hide behind,
stanza after stanza, line after line but ...
Why am I blind to myself, until myself is on paper?
Though I was never even gone.
My right hand lived on while I disappeared
and I couldn't tell any longer, what the words ended up saying.
When I write where do I go? Really? I guess I'll never know.

With Time
by Darleen Bruno

Oh those wonderful moments we shared
Back then it was too common to care
But somehow along the way
Our relationship was led astray
I try to forgive as God has done for me
But it's easier said than done, that holy decree
Because I know these chains of unforgiveness will only hold me down
But after how you've treated me, I think I'd rather drown
So, after everything you've done with no sense of remorse
I might as well just let time run its course
Because if the clock hand hitting twelve declares the end
Who am I to fight against it and try to make amends
However, I can't help but think when I glimpse into the past,
If only I knew that time I loved you might be the last

Crushed Dreams
by Susanna Denny

Last night, I had a dream in which I could be anyone, anything I wanted to be.
Such is the promise made to me:
"Life, liberty, and the pursuit of happiness."
Those are my rights, rights of freedom and independence.
This morning, I woke up in a world where those are not my rights,
they are my privileges.
I woke up in a world unwilling to give others what is given to me.
I woke up in a world where life may unexpectedly meet its end
at the hands of those trusted to secure it.
I woke up in a world where too many are deprived
of the basic liberties they deserve.
I woke up in a world where happiness is only for those who can afford it.
I woke up, I woke up, and that was my first mistake.

Friction From the Heart
by Bradley Ellis

I can't help but stare at the carpet.
It's fascinating, how each pigmented bundle of fiber is rooted together,
uniform and shoulder to shoulder.
There's no breathing room, like a permanent bus ride
in New York City during New Year's Eve.
And I pity each and every head, patiently waiting.
My mom always said that one of my biggest flaws is being too empathetic,
and that being too considerate in a slick world will be the epitome of my downfall.
I am someone who is hesitant and craves to be perceived as flawless.
But oddly enough I am no reflection of my philosophy,
as I am known by most for my arrogance and naive banter.
I am truly a paradox,
I'm someone incapable of making friends as much as I am of keeping them.

Screens
by Caterina Dottino

Her retinas burn
saturated colors assault her nerves
she hides herself in a dark room
for now, all she needs to do is scroll
the outside world ceases to exist
blending into a colorless blur around her
as her half-lidded eyes struggle to focus on the screen
her mind is filled with cotton
and her neck aches from the folded pillow wedged under it
who is she? she doesn't remember
but she thinks she wouldn't like her
so she presses delete
and wakes up.

My Father's Only Daughter
by Jacqueline Bodycomb

I am my father's only daughter
I want to change the world more than I want to be liked
I want to make the world better, but get frustrated I cannot
I scream when I am upset
I wield his rage to get my way, not realizing it has become my own
I wear his anger like it is a hand-me-down jacket
I wish I could throw it out
I don't like the way the material feels against my skin, heavy and suffocating
I hate how ridiculous I look and that everyone knows it's far too big on me
I resent how, no matter what,
it stays in the back of my closet waiting to be pulled out again
I am my father's only daughter
And what kind of daughter returns "a gift"

Things I Didn't Want To Know
by Ella Gonzales

I didn't want to know about the hatred people have towards one another.
Or about the hatred Mother Nature has towards us.
I didn't want to know how the glaciers are
drip
drip
dripping
Like tears down those children's faces
while they sit under their desks listening for the shots to ring out.
Anticipating death.
I didn't want to know about the buildings tumbling down,
like the blocks I used to play with.
Children losing their childhoods to air raids.
I didn't want to know about the loss, the hatred and disaster.
The only thing I wanted to know was the comfort of my ignorance.

Hunting
by Jedadiah Ballard

Crack! It is a gun
Thud the animal drops dead
Hunting is so fun

Pocket of Sunshine
by Cristiana McCoy

My days are dark
My nights are gloomy
My days are rainy
My nights are thundering
Day after day I'm led astray from who I am and how I feel.
But him
He's so different, he's so pure, full of happiness, what is he waiting for.
His days are bright
His nights are warm
His days are sunny
His nights have no mourn
When he smiles I do turn red, He let me see myself again.
When our hands meet and when we touch
We than grinned, we never have enough
When I'm with him I never thought I'd feel
My happiness grow stronger than the dark
I realize I now only have happiness in my heart.

Smile
by Lorenzo Martinez

A smile can bring a breath of life
Few people think so
Or they try to hide it and look away
But just one smile can help in day and night
We always want to smile at any moment
We smile for happiness
We also smile for every emotion
The meaning behind it can impact another's life
A smile can leave from a feeling or a death
A lot of people say they have nothing left
When they see another happy, they look away
They cannot hide that they long for the feeling once more
It can leave and go at any moment without you knowing It
During covid we couldn't see what was underneath
When we couldn't see them, we don't feel cheerful
When we don't smile, we don't feel free
A simple smile is a way of communicating
You won't know the feeling unless you take the first step
It's a few muscles movements from your mouth
From sunrise to sundown

Little Peaco
by Mariah Massari

How a boost of serotonin
travels up my brain
every time I look
through the distorted glass bowl
How your bright colors
flow through the water so elegantly
I'm almost jealous that
that can't be me
You live such a simple life
yet you turn so many heads
I want that simple life
and to live in that little bowl instead

Cyberbullying
by Gabriela Lucas

Creating a post for all people to see
You get love and support from all your friends and family
But, behind those screens there are a billion people
Beating you down because they are evil
Ruthless comments and hatred begin to show
By yourself you then start to feel alone
Unexpected people start to report
Last of the haters continue to "support"
Laughing and sharing not knowing its wrong
You sit there alone, believing all their lies
Instead of raising your chin up high
Neglecting the real beauty you have inside
Get up and stand up for those who feel left behind

My Cat
by Celeste Quintana

She is a loving cat with fur as soft as clouds
She wakes me up at night, meowing so loud
With beautiful yellow eyes that blaze at night
She's a chunky cat that lights my life
With hope and company when no one was keeping me company
Her fur feels so rich beneath my fingertips
Hearing her stomps while she hangs around the house
Seeing her sleep peacefully and waiting for me to get home
She loves to be carried and given so many treats
She's the happiest cat I've ever seen
She bumps me with her head to let me know I'm not alone
I've never met a sweeter cat than her
She's been my comfort ever since she was born
Keeping me calm when no one could
She's the reminder I need to get up in the mornings

Please Stay, Summer
by Morgan Fowler

Amiably soaking up the sunshine
Surrounded with an aroma of felicity
The welcoming presence of loved ones that warms our souls
Savoring these moments that are rare but enduring
Nostalgia for what has been
Anxiety for the persistent future beckoning to come
Trying to hold onto to these fleeting moments
that feel as though they are already memories
But, for now, we lounge agreeably with adoration
For the ability to be in this present moment
Unable to accept the inescapable but ever present fact
That all good things must come to a bittersweet end.

Voyage
by Shyla Salmon

We're all sailing on a boat
Floating, searching the horizon for a destination
Insecurity paving our path of motion for us
Waves of pressure forcing us to conform,
Tides of dreams never chased and later turned into regrets,
We must realize sooner that we are all in control of our own boat
We can steer and travel the path to our deepest desires
We stay trapped in stormy waters,
riddled with pressure, regret, insecurity and broken dreams
We become immensely afraid at the idea of sailing a sea not traveled
But once we take control of our boat and steer our own path through the storm,
We can survive the storm and live the life of our dreams

The Old Brick Building
by Paige Storment

An old brick building on 19th street
Where my childhood memories lie
Countless hours spent staring out of my bedroom
Just looking at the sky
When I think of the ivy climbing up the walls
I wonder if it reached the top
For as burgeoning as ivy is eventually,
It has to stop
My old home on 19th street
With its creaky boards and thin walls
As I walk past it
I wish just for one more time to walk around in its magnificent halls
For the old brick building on 19th street
It's where my childhood memories stay
And even though I miss it dearly
I must carry on for another day

A Galaxy Filled With Pines
by Claire Elise Rasmussen

My heart is a pine
Sharp and protected ...
The savory inside
Softly unexpected ...
Just one hug away from
Reconnected ...
One needle at a time.
Your heart is a galaxy
Filled with a soft stardusting ...
The veins a glittering glow
Its fragments lusting ...
For the simple pines below.

Unsanctifying Grace
by Isabelle Duprey

A lunar driven attraction, at the ascending apex of the solstice,
this evening; an evening for the ages.
The dames of the abominable craft
come together as one. Hand in hand,
laced in moranian silks, adorned with impish holly.
Wavering the scent of frankincense and myrrh as they prowl.
Idle of the infernal divine that awaits to beseech them with power and glory;
so the tale goes. Solely this nevermore.
Brave is she, a maiden of silver and gold,
thine beauty shines of the Gods of Old.
Oh precious naive Lenore who dared to be, ever so bold
Fate sewed sealed, she is no more.

Land of Echoes
by Kimberly Johnson

Sitting high on the mountains we cry
yet the mountains cry back
It is only then you may realize
they were crying first
You merely gave them a voice
on which to scream
Ponder not the world you made
rather what world you made for
Why are you crying?
For I am no wolf
No howl was mine
yet I sang their song
What have you moved?
For the trees dance alone
I was once an echo
Though I became the wind

Where
by Amelia Diminico

I have often wondered.
I have often looked.
I have taken the road less traveled.
I have traveled rigorously so.
I have searched for myself in all of these places
and in all of these places I fall short
I have watched the days go dimmer as the happiness lies
on the floor I sit and on the floor I die

The Trials of Nature
by Abigail Roth

The Beautiful fish in the sea uphold honor and devotion
The bright Hyacinths happily leap in the breeze
The graceful tree in the cemetery endures the grandeur of many burials
Dawn rises on the stream,
Bringing a soft rain that lulls the sleeping man into his death
And that bright, shimmering evening,
As the man rises to heaven,
A stranger in the distance is watching,
Cheering him on as he continues to his next life.

Solitude
by Eliana Smith

"Learn to love solitude"
And, to love you.
You, you that is true
Even if she is blue
Please remember she has grew,
from the child that never knew what the world had in store
beyond her bedroom door,
Whether it was in her pocket or her drawer
Ever since she was four her light always found
its way through every cracked door
to heal even if it was just her mothers back,
a back that has been lead, in dread,
never not in her head,
curled up alone in her bed but barely even fed,
feeling dead she'd shed the words the world has read
that have cracked her back and torn her skin
telling her it's nearly impossible for her to win.
"Learn to love solitude" my mom would say
Late in the day when the sweet air flowed through the walk way
I wondered why she is this way
"learn to love solitude my mom would say"
I realized then solitude is the only thing my mother has ever known.

True Love
by Michelle Katz

A piece of me
I give to you,
No matter I'm 5 or 32.
I give you flowers to say "I love you"
I give you hugs to show my love.
I throw you hearts from up above.
I kiss your lips to show true love.
I stand behind you like a wall,
Ready to fight through it all.

Mania
by Kezia Lawrence

Unashamedly your slave
Bound and enthralled
Breathless with the ecstasy of effortless love
In a state of deliria
Forever seeking your approval
Clawing away to be the only one you set your gaze upon
Dependent on the feeling, the way your cold soul scorches my very being
Helpless and defenseless, your divinity giving strength
Obsession, intoxication, addicted to a ruthless goddess

Friday Night in the Kitchen
by Carolina Rosciglione

After school, a short brisk walk
Up the steps, in the door, into The Kitchen.
The Kitchen where everyone gathers
Where we gossip over brownies, cupcakes, cookies
Where we laugh until we are on the floor crying
Where we speak out truths
Unravel our trauma, our drama
Grab two slices of sicilian from the pie on the stove,
Grab three ice cubes from the broken ice machine,
fill the water in the fridge door
We all sit down, eat and play Banana Grams
or Telestrations or Monopoly or Taboo
Yesterday it was a Friday in eighth grade, and we debated about Team Spirit.
Today it's the first day of junior year, and we're complaining about
homework and crazy teachers.
Tomorrow it will be the last day of senior year,
and we're committed to college and celebrating
what we hope is not our last Friday in The Kitchen.
We have changed, yet we are the same
The new paint on the walls and new fridge with a working ice machine
cannot change the sanctuary that is The Kitchen

Thalassophilia
by April Ramirez

Her azure waves and turquoise tide
Did yet surround me still
Yet I did not panic nor try to flee
As my lungs began to fill
And as she pulled me deeper
Into her depths below
I held my breath and closed my eyes,
For finally, I was home.

Hidden Feelings
by Rylee Kinney

I am the class clown
I am the person you come to if you need a good laugh
I am the one that will sit there for however long you need me
I am the one that is always there but after all that
I am also the one left out
I am the last person to be asked "hey how are you doing?"
I am the class clown I never have a bad day
Right?
Oh how they were wrong
I am the one to make you laugh so that both of our days can be better
I am not only the class clown
I am human

I Don't Want To Look For You In Rainbows
by Laila Mansour

I don't want to look for you in rainbows,
In painted dreams across the sky;
I don't want to think of you in heartache,
And with the sprinkler droplets cry.
I don't want to look for you in fireworks,
In the flames of color in the sky;
I don't want to hear you in piano melodies,
Praising the Lord on high.
I don't want to look for you in sunsets,
Watching the sun fall across the sky;
I don't want to be reminded
Of the limits of time.
I don't want to look for you in objects,
I want to look you in the eyes.
I want to be feel your warm embrace,
Here on Earth, not in the sky.
I want to say goodbye.

Forever and Always
by Angelina Borg

I often ask what I did to deserve you
The one who always gets me through.
You helped me see
The goodness in this cruel world.
You brought warmth,
To my coldest,
Most lonesome places.
It has been a privilege,
To know and adore you.
And when this is all over,
I'll be thankful I knew you,
Forever and always.

To Live Again
by Jennifer Baker

Visit me! Oh, sweet Death.
Let me feel your kiss.
Take me in your open arms.
Envelope me in your touch.
I cannot carry on dear Death!
The pain is all too real!
I feel myself slip away with every passing day.
Yet still you hide in shadows and mystery,
Your face doomed to be hidden.
Darling Death! Set me free!
Into my final paradise, to run and be released.

She
by Olivia Hodge

Perfection only ever graced me once
A fire solely made to burn for me
My thoughts redundant every day for months
For I was helplessly entranced by she
In such a short time, she met great renown
Her skin of peach, but most of all her hair
Those auburn locks could a forest burn down
A conflagration, no one could compare
How I regret my tendency to wait
Forbidden fruit I took too long to bite
She had the pride to title me 'too late'
Though years have passed, she haunts my every night
I'm left to know what I will never know
The fire I refused to burn ago

Secrets In Plain Sight
by Kaida Dee

In the depths of the forest floor,
Amidst the damp and the decay,
A hidden world of wonder,
A blessing to the Earth, they say.
Fungi, in all their glory,
A kingdom of shapes and hues,
From the tiny to the towering,
A world of knowledge to pursue.
Some are red and white, like toadstools,
Others brown and earthy-toned,
Some are shaped like delicate cups,
Others like umbrellas, finely honed.
Fungi, they are a mystery,
A puzzle yet to be solved,
A source of wonder and delight,
A treasure to beheld.
Whether they grow in sunny fields,
Or in the depths of the wood,
Mushrooms are a thing of beauty,
A gift from nature, pure and good.

A Season's Sacrifice
by Scarlett Kingston

If a thought invades my trying for slumber
Or memories meddle in the warmness of Summer
Winter, callous and jealousy asunder
Will call upon a Fall encumbered
Where brisk billows, indiscriminate, rampage and plunder
Spring, free-flowingly pious and interceding
Took upon the burdens of its siblings, pleading
Yet, Winter, vexed and distressed of their sweeting
Closed its ears in favor of competing
Where sleep is lost, stale, and fleeting
Summer, stagnantly beared the sheath of cold unkind
Insipid through Winter's cruel and partisan pride
Fall began to regret the scruple's bind
Sheepishly awaiting its siblings incline
Yet, Summer's renewal, an unsure prospect, failed to mind
The lasting bitterness from Winter spread
A sacrificial Spring gave up its last warmth ahead
Through selfless favor, Summer evaded its dread
They lay dormant, breathless, not yet dead
And I wake restless in my tepid bed

"True" Flight
by Athina Protonentis

As a baby bird, I sang an endless song.
My cheeks, as red as a strawberry.
My eyes like a camera,
Clear and veracious.
Dancing and waving as I went,
I had no cares on that day.
Oh, how much has changed?
With each passing second, my song is subdued.
With each passing minute,
I am losing you.
I feel a weight on my chest,
Stealing notes from my tongue,
The waters of life drowning out my lungs.
I need a mirror to see, but I have lost my sight.
The smart told me stories; the dumb told me lies.
And I kept quiet.
Till the songbird I was, became dark inside.
As questions and comments battered and bruised,
I became a crow
Because I believed in your "truths."

A Tale of Two Trees
by Madeline Anderson

I look at the man before me, a reflection of a better me;
I despise his cleanly cut face, his chestnut hair in ribbon.
He leans toward the sun, absorbing her radiant beams,
While I am left with nothing but pitiable specks.
I wither and wilt underneath the wine-dark sky,
And yet for him, the heavens never cease to shine.
How am I meant to be a flame and a light
When I am flickering and faltering?
Now the axe is being sharpened,
Its glaring eye on him.
Will the sun still shine without the whispering of his leaves
Or will we be the last to feel her warm embrace?
The logger draws nearer as I fear for the tundra soon to be.
Then it comes to me that maybe I cannot be a flame
But I can be kindling.
I am filled with peace I have never felt before
Even with my head below the guillotine,
Knowing that the sun will forever glow.
I relish the last of her touch
As the axe falls and I am redeemed.

In That Time
by Troy Larner

In that time ...
People liked to whine
Not because they wanted too,
but because they chose to.
Not for attention,
but to get attention.
Not for words of affirmation,
but for the feeling of affirmation.
Not for comfort,
but to have the feeling of comfort.
In that time,
people chose violence,
not for fun,
but for the feeling they "can".
Not for change,
but to change the ways of people.
Not to feel secure,
but to have the feeling of security.
In that time ...
People changed.

Like the Ocean
by Ashley Keneth

My father admired me the way I now admire the ocean.
The power and clarity it holds.
How it has the ability to shine a light of beauty and create a great storm.
I listen to the waves crashing against the sand like an extravagant lion's roar!
My father's imperfect hands hold me tight.
Protecting me from any danger that may come my way.
His abrasive hold makes me feel safe, like no one could hurt me.
I feel his affection and his hands are a comfortable sensation,
as he always holds my hand wherever we go.
I look at my dad with a smile on my face
in aspiration hoping one day, I can be just like him.
Charmful, intelligent and funny.
With no clue in the world how drastically
our relationship would change.
And how greatly 17 year old me would treasure to relive this moment again.
With his recognizable, black, rectangle glasses that darken in the sun.
I wonder what it would be like to see the world through his glasses.
Maybe I could understand my father or
For my dad to admire me
like how I now admire the ocean.

Tips Up
by Ezekiel McGee

Snow spread like a sheet over mountains of white
Strengthening sun melts the cold of the night
Burst out, gear up, and bundle up tight
Together creating an affair to excite
Equipment-laid shoulders march to the hill
A half-mile slog, testing the will
Keen balance required so as not to spill
All for the sport, all for the thrill
Slap down the skis - pure anticipation
Hassle? Yes, but a worthy operation
Click in the bindings with pent-up sensation
Slide into line, a chaotic formation
Up and away, swept by spindly lifts
Cool mountain breeze, most refreshing of gifts
Flying above shadow-cast drifts
Splayed over pine trees, boulders, and rifts
Hum of the station heard through tall trees
Bar lifted, tips up as chairs slow to ease
Onto groomed paths stretching far as eyes see
These are the moments I feel most free

To Be Black
by Annabel Adun

Oh, to be black
Were we ever truly free?
Or is that just the narrative society forces us to believe
Oh, to be black
To rap and dance like no other race
To bring life, even to a boring place
Oh, to be black
To be discriminated against
Wrongfully sent to jails, beaten and bruised
Until we're forced to repent
Oh, to be black
Radiant with natural beauty
Clear skin, that's often filled with melanin
Oh, to be black
Expected to fail
Having to work ten times harder, in order to prevail
Oh, to be black
The biggest challenge you'll ever receive
A life chosen for you, with no guaranteed way of knowing you'll succeed
Oh, to be black!

Mi Corazón
by Ganjina Haitova

A broken heart
Which you shattered
The cuts of deception
Have left a stain
Tanto deseo que
Los pensamientos
De ti se me irían
If only you could see
The pain that was left
In my heart, the cuts
Tan profundas que
La espada sigue ahí
They the cuts
Don't want to heal
The blood it seeps
Como un reloj de arena
Del que gotea la sangre
Mi amor por ti es
Como una hermosa maldición

Dreams of a Madman
by Joshua Motielall

It is late July and I am starting to wonder why
Many nights I look up at the sky feeling angry and wanting to cry
I don't believe I have the ability to fly high
I wake up wondering who to blame
Everytime this makeshift plan goes to flames
My mind just starts to play games
Not this time though I think I've done it
I sit and ponder all of the outcomes, until I get that hit
No more mistakes, I finally realized that this fits
I take off this disguise and surprise all of the wondering eyes
I was never done saying all of my goodbyes
It should never have been a surprise, my hard work would eventually comply
I've been chasing fake smiles looking for affection
Turns out I was looking in the wrong direction
Like everyone else I'm full of imperfections
I was giving off a surreal reflection
Offering a profound mystic that makes me live at my peak
This cynical mindset of the public was a unique technique
Now I can live in peace with no more critiques

The Agony of Deserted Dreamer
by Cassandra Trujillo

She flies too close to me,
I get too jealous at times.
Even though you don't want me,
I still think you're mine.
You blow the fire in me,
But you refuse to blow it out.
I do want some feeling,
But in my heart there's a drought.
Nobody steal my light,
It's been so dim tonight.
You want to leave me in love,
You must know it's not right.
I've lost a gamble with love, and it hurts.
When it looks like you might move on,
I hear the cries of doves, and it lurks.
My deep desire, my only dream,
Left only to my memories.
My one attraction, The apple of my eye,
Wants to desert me.

3 PM
by Harmony Lewis

You deserved a kinder goodbye
One filled with lustrous flowers and stuffed bears
With childhood stories and board games
And long nights surrounded by family
I wished to snuggle up
On your hospital bed you, crippled by age
And see your way out
Into a kinder place
Not get a call at 3 PM
Too young
You deserved to feel cherished on your way out
Or perhaps that's the selfish thing I tell myself
As I long for a goodbye I didn't get
Advice you no longer tell
A wedding you won't attend
You loved the rain; I drench myself
When a life so cruel as yours ends
A kinder goodbye ought to be permitted
But there's no rainbow after the rain.

Life Behind a Wall
by Olivia Shirk

You live behind a wall.
There are no stones,
nor metal or fencing
but a screen.
Behind a screen that
hides
who you truly are.
Hides the flaws,
insecurities,
and the mistakes.
Hides the fears
and the tears.
You hide who you are,
but so do I.
I hide that I am not perfect,
my flaws and imperfections.
I to live behind a wall.

I Think I've Fallen In Love
by Airlea Deutscher

I thought I fell in love once,
with a boy of six years with long eyelashes and a cheesy smile.
I guess my heart saw something my head didn't.
I told the boy when I was seven that I knew a princess,
and she gave him make-believe golden shoes. He played along.
Years passed and what I thought was my love for him
faded away, although I still thought of him sometimes.
I thought of him when I thought of marriage,
and when I asked myself if I wanted
a prince or a princess. He moved along.
I think I've fallen in love now,
with a moonlight angel who I swim in the night with
and whose eyes are brown like his were.
And I know now that she is something that he wasn't,
I don't know why.
I tell the girl that I'm a writer,
and then I give her stories that she'll never hear again.
She is not a princess, and neither am I.
I don't think I need a fairy-tale anymore.

Spiders In My Skin
by Elise Neal

Spiders in my skin
Crawling out my ears,
Slipping down my neck,
Creeping through my shoulder blades,
And tumbling down my back.
Smacking, crunching;
Clapping, whistling;
Snapping, coughing;
They spook the spiders
And they scatter all about.
Flick them from my wrists,
Shoot them from my fingers.
Shake them from my head,
And pull their webs from my hair.
They drip into my eyes
And now I can't see.
Keep shaking and shaking
But the spiders in my skin never leave.

Best Friends
by Nevaeh Smith

I used to hate her
When I ask myself why I did it's a blur
She is good with art
It's why she is so smart
I love the highlights in her hair
And how it smells like fresh air
She has eyes that shine
They look like deep purple wine
She is scared of dogs
Even though she has dogs
She hates liars
Even more the spiders
She wears lots of hoodies
When she gets a new one she says "oh goodie!"
She has boy problems
But she is never the problem
I love her so much
I think I'm gonna take her to lunch

Adrift
by Kamronbek Kalimbetov

A midnight, an intense river-stream,
With dense forest lining,
With a peaceful feeling,
I drift atop the water's surface.
Still awake and floating,
Still adrift atop the river,
Still under the shining moonlight,
Still afloat, on the river's surface.
Under the river's surface,
Oh the peaceful stream-bed,
Oh the sunken solace,
How I wish to rot below it.
Yet I cannot sink,
Still on the river's surface,
Still carried atop the flow,
Still another failed attempt.
Under the river's surface,
Oh the peaceful stream-bed,
Oh the sunken solace,
"Maybe next time"

Habromania
by Angelina Laibhen

We were always taught that we are damned if we do and damned if we don't
All of this just seems so cutthroat
The sigh of a hypocrite dies over the course of a day
A sucker is born every minute, but who are we to blame
The course of a life shouldn't have a price
But capitalism always makes up think twice
Will Earth be a paradise ever again?
Should we restart and go back to the days in Eden?
Are we out of our minds for straying further from the truth
Or perhaps everything is just coming full circle like they always do
Childhood innocence that never strayed
Muddy shoes from being caught in the rain
Processions for those who died, and
Accomplishments for a life we've gained
We already take so much for granted
But now the seeds of doubt are planted
Will it be squandered as per usual
But just for once humanity will have a change of heart
To be a bit less typical and embrace a brand new start

Footprints
by Dylan Jackson

thin snowy fleece comforts frozen ground.
footprints first to roam the trail.
thin branches slouch due to weight of snow.
snow melts from sun's ardor.
beads of water glisten mid-air.
aroma of pine fills the lungs.
breath waltzes upon exhale.
my mind begins to wander.
pondering the process of progression.
frostnip to frostbite
freezing to frigid
fluid to frozen
i stop.
mind no longer moving.
legs no longer thinking.
frozen in place.
for bitter wind swoops in.
sky begins to flurry.

Good and Bad
by Marabella Zaldivar

My God is good
My God is Love
The evil of this world, that does not come from my God
The evil will not be overcome by crystals and candles
while controlling your breaths
But will only and has only been overcome by Jesus
The sun brings joy and the rain brings sorrow
The Son brings joy the enemy brings sorrow
He the Son my God Jesus Christ has brought me an abundance of love and joy
Jesus is the good
satan my enemy is the bad
he is against my brothers and sisters and I
he brings this world hate
While Jesus brought this world salvation and love
Just as I'm sure the sun has risen this morning
I am sure the Son of God has risen and is alive
I have nothing without my God
And for everything I am able to do and say
including these words it is through Him
Glory be to God

Untitled
by Kourtney White

i exude a radiance of sunshine
a pure, kind soul
a sweet spirited person
then i met you,
you fed me lies
distracted me from what i am here for
i thought you loved me
you broke me.
the heart has to be broken to be opened
so, did you really break me?
you helped me become the person that i am today
your lies are why i am stronger
i still exude a radiance of sunshine
a purer, kinder soul
a sweeter spirited person
i met you, loved you, left you
i am healed now

A Human Experience
by Samantha Workman

I have felt misfortune often, some that I
Will feel once more, or felt in mind
Not ever shall I be fully healed of it
Be it not wrong to always struggle?
Trampled by people with eyes pointed ahead
Again with their cutting acts opening old wounds
For they cannot see the pain they cause
I see it far too clearly
Have I been unkind? Surely, for pain begets pain
Grown up now, I can prevent myself from scarring
No beloved of mine will face what I have fought
Longer still I will have to wait
Shall I ever stop waiting?
I do not think so
Be it hours or days or weeks or years
Made anew I will assuredly be
A human with scars, ascended above mortality
Fool, a phrase I know means A Beginning
I'm alive and I'm better than ever before
Free I am now, and free I shall forever be.

Anxiety
by Isabella Masterson

On the outside, you are beautifully dressed
Happy, cheerful, and bright
But on the inside you are doing your best
To keep the demons inside out of sight
My nail polish chipped away
My lips all tough
My body astray
I've had enough
Exhaustion
Fatigued
My eyes frosted
As people tried to bring me relief
Exhaustion
Fatigue
Exhaustion
Fatigue
Too much for me
Just let me be

The Pawn
by Connor Darouvar

Since I was little, the one thing I've been sold
Abandon hopes, abandon dreams, invest all time and gold
But to stop this skewed fate, I've been forced to embrace
This almighty god, I defy in this case
For I have devoted every ounce of my time
Yet am always skimmed over by your all-seeing eye
So I stand before you, not beneath or above
For I have no disrespect, yet no ounce of love
You give me my all, my brain, and my heart
But you allow it to break as you keep us apart
You give the world life, and you may give it meaning
But for all fun and games, you cease that life's gleaming
I have no more yearn to be let through that gate
As through your pettiness, you consume me with hate
Though you may be all-seeing, you will never see me
For you reap what you sow, and are not above thee
Have I made myself clear? Because I now rest my case
You are no god to me, and not who I replaced

What My Mirror Stands For
by Ellie Ortiz Mendoza

My outer appearance.
Is this how I look now?
Reminiscing the past.
Retouching my face.
Observing the work of time.
Regretting.

Rotten Nectarine
by Ece Ozel

A rotten fruit
Battered and bruised
Was high and beautiful on the tree
Now returns yet again to the ground
Innards gone out
Will go on to nourish its way back on top
But shall yet again return to the forest floor
Stardust to stardust
Ashes to ashes
What goes up must return down
And what's down will eventually go up
It's the cycle of life
Plucked too early
Or
Left to rot on the branch

Shame
by Kat Taylor

Your shame is art
It's sad and heart wrenching
Yet still it is art
It glimmers with the light of the sun
Yet like Icarus you too did fall
My shame is shame
It is just dull and useless pain
Agony built up from days long gone
Empty feelings of loneliness turned to dark unyielding pain
Shame can be art
You showed me that
I too wish to fly to the sun and surpass the stars
I long to have shame that glimmers in daylight yet still glows by the moon
You make shame art
You can twist my shame into paintings
You can manipulate my pain to make it shine
It is not the shame that is art but artist who uses shame
I wish one day to spin shame to gold

Ode To a Shining Star
by Gavin Vander Schaaf

O shining star,
O great light within the ever-reaching darkness,
Your luminescence penetrates to the deepest crevice of my iris.
Might you be a vast planet or a blazing sun or an omnipotent god?
Might you look down on us meager humans
As one looks down on a dog on the street?
Might you laugh,
When upon this living rock,
The inconsequential pets that wander around
Fret about, believing that their troubles
Matter much in this grand universe that they call home?
O star,
When a love fades to grey,
Or a civilization crumble,
Do you too fret?
No, you sit upon your throne of black space
Guessing at the length of time that shall pass
Whereupon the next human will see the great forest among the trees.
O star,
What say you of me,
Pondering, Staring, Glaring, Seeking, Wishing,
Sneering, Watching, Reaching, After you?
Or is it foolish,
Is it foolish to merely believe
That you, O star,
Might even take notice?
I sit upon this bench,
Searching for answers that will not come,
Reaching after you, day by day,
And I've come only to realize one thing.
I will not ever reach you.
And I believe that for the best.
Because, O star,
Though my questions on this rock
May hold no priority over you
Though my thoughts may never see the light of fruition
Though my actions may never cause the tides to crash
The trees to grow
Or the wind to sway as I so desire
I have found some comfort.
O star,
It is clear that in reaching for you, I have found my light.

3rd Place

Liana Giannuzzi

Nostalgia
by Liana Giannuzzi

In awe was I mimicking my Nonna's motions
Molding pasta into my favorite shape.
Piece by piece, one by one, intricate, handmade,
With tender care, an Italian's passion.
I sat there as a beam of radiant light, reflecting off her.
The flower printed apron covered her carefully selected outfit,
The joy in my eyes as her ways endowed me,
Her arms stretch to reach my hand.
So focused on her craft, extending it to a girl whom she loved.
And I know her eyes, beaming with inspiration and a soft grin.
Gentle in her ways yet the strongest woman
who would soon endure a battle rather tough.
Before God would wrap his arms around her,
The way she used to wrap them around me.
But this time he would never let go.
And still today,
If I close my eyes just tight enough,
When I reach out my hand
Her arms meet mine and show me the way.
And there I am again, making pasta in her kitchen.

Madeline Lacotts

No Longer a Kid On Christmas Eve
by Madeline Lacotts

Your journal haunts me, because I know it's written for me.
Dad's thrown it in his closet, lying beneath shoes,
fallen hangers, a hospital bag.
Everything I need is in that journal,
but I'd hate to spoil the calamity of not knowing.
My fingers tremble, tracing the pages
flitting against my fingernail.
Your ring on my right hand,
Dad's ring on the other.
His ring, because he's alive and yours, because you're not.
Just like Christmas Eve.
I'd kneel in Mom and Dad's closet,
run my hands over each gift,
fidget with each bow.
Now it's your journal, Mom, in Dad's closet.
No matter how much it taunts me, the pages stay closed.
You know I'd never open gifts until Christmas Morning.

1st Place

Carson Kramer

This year's Editor's Choice Award
and a total of $600 in prize money goes to Carson Kramer.
Now a senior, Carson's poem, "Mother"
is a sobering picture of what many teenagers face
during what can be their most challenging years.
Yet, a ray of hope, in the form of a mother's love,
can shine in even the darkest of places.
Well done, Carson!

Editor's Choice Award

Mother
by Carson Kramer

I have stepped on this welcome mat before
But I will never be able to do it again
I have heard the microwave beeping for me
Just one more time than I should have
I have sat at the same turning chair
Every night of my life, every night I've been able to remember
There are dents engraved in the wood
From how many times I've spun into the table
The corners of the playing cards are folded
From my hands, that were much smaller once before
My mother smiles at me in the kitchen, scrunching her nose
And I fall to the ground.
Not because of the pills in my stomach
But because I know that if they were there
I would never be able to see her do that again
So I smile back and run upstairs
I crumble up the letter I have beautifully written
And I take the prescription I have stolen
And I pour it down the drain, tears in my eyes
I don't do it, for my mother's smile.

Index of Authors

Index of Authors

Index of Authors

Index of Authors

Index of Authors